D1567447

POSITIVE LIBERTY

MELBOURNE INTERNATIONAL PHILOSOPHY SERIES

VOLUME 7

POSITIVE LIBERTY

by

LAWRENCE CROCKER

Communications to be addressed to the Editor, c/o Philosophy Department, University of Melbourne, Parkville, 3052, Victoria, Australia.

POSITIVE LIBERTY

An Essay in Normative Political Philosophy

by

LAWRENCE CROCKER

1980

MARTINUS NIJHOFF PUBLISHERS

THE HAGUE / BOSTON / LONDON

Distributors:

for the United States and Canada

Kluwer Boston, Inc.
160 Old Derby Street
Hingham, MA 02043
USA

for all other countries

Kluwer Academic Publishers Group
Distribution Center
P.O. Box 322
3300 AH Dordrecht
The Netherlands

Library of Congress Cataloging in Publication Data CIP

Crocker, Lawrence.
    Positive liberty.

    (Melbourne international philosophy series; v. 7)
    Includes bibliographical references.
    1. Liberty. I. Title. II. Series.
JC585.C74   323.44'01   79-28437

ISBN 90–247–2291–8 (this volume)
ISBN 90–247–2331–0 (series)

PRINTED IN THE NETHERLANDS

To the memory of my wife

JANE ELIZABETH ENGLISH

who was killed climbing the Matterhorn, September 11, 1978. She made important contributions to philosophy and feminism, and taught, by example, the joy of living.

ACKNOWLEDGEMENT

This essay was made possible by a sabbatical grant from the University of Washington and by the hospitality of the Philosophy Department of the University of North Carolina at Chapel Hill which provided research facilities. I am indebted to many colleagues and friends for valuable suggestions, among them Robert Coburn, David Crocker, Steven Darwall, Gerald Dworkin, Jane English, Dan Lyons, and Robert Richman. I also wish to thank the editors of *The Personalist*, now the *Pacific Philosophical Quarterly*, for their permission to reprint 'Coercion and the Wage Agreement,' which appears here as Section 6, and was originally printed in Volume 59 of *The Personalist*.

LAWRENCE CROCKER

CONTENTS

CHAPTER I

INTRODUCTION

Liberty is perhaps the most praised of all social ideals. Rare is the modern political movement which has not inscribed "liberty," "freedom," "liberation," or "emancipation" prominently on its banners. Rarer still is the political leader who has spoken out against liberty, though, of course, some have condemned "license." While there is overwhelming agreement on the value of liberty, however, there is a great deal of disagreement on what liberty is. It is this fact that explains how it is possible for the most violently opposed of political parties to pay homage to the "same" ideal.

From among the many ways liberty is understood, this essay will be concerned with only two. The first takes liberty to be the absence of human interference with the individual's actions. This is the way liberty has been understood by the Anglo-American "liberal" tradition from Thomas Hobbes in the seventeenth century to J.S. Mill in the nineteenth to such contemporary, and very dissimilar, political philosophers as John Rawls and Robert Nozick. The "absence of interference" school is far from monolithic in its understanding of liberty, but it is united in its opposition to a rival account on which liberty is not taken to be the absence of human interference but rather the presence of diverse possibilities or opportunities. So, very roughly, the first account describes liberty in terms of what an individual is not kept from doing by other people; the second describes liberty in terms of what the individual can do. For obvious reasons, these two different accounts have come to be called "negative" and "positive" respectively, although, as we will see shortly, this terminology has sometimes led to confusion.

The division among political philosophers on positive and negative liberty reflects, though only roughly, differences with respect to political sympathies as well. Positive libertarians tend to stand politically to the left of their negative counterpart. One important strain within the negative tradition is concerned, almost exclusively, with limiting government. Laws, bureaucracies, and centralized power are taken to be the chief sources of the interference that destroys freedom. For these negative libertarians, the working generalization is the less government the better. (Probably no one believes that *every* reduction of government is an increase in liberty. For example, it is uncontroversial that a cut in the police budget would not enlarge liberty if it led to a massive wave of kidnappings.) It goes almost without saying, that the private property market economy is taken by most anti-government libertarians to be the core of a free society.

Let me emphasize that while these *laissez faire* politics represent a well-defined and historically influential pole within the negative tradition, there are many negative libertarians whose politics are very different. Not all negative libertarians are hostile to government regulation of the economy, even to the point of large scale income redistribution. Some are even open to socialism. But typically redistributionist liberals and socialists tend towards a positive conception of liberty.

The positive libertarian is concerned that people are often prevented from doing things, not by laws or direct interference, but by matters whose roots lie deep in the institutional structure of the society. The welfare mother who is legally free to vacation on Corfu, but who barely has the wherewithal to get across town, is a typical case. She cannot vacation on Corfu, even if the reasons for her financial incapacity turn on the nature of the economy and are not naturally called "interferences." Similarly, the blind man is not interfered with by those who could afford to pay for a sight-restoring operation. But because he goes without the operation, what he can do is significantly limited.

The positive tradition, then, tends to go hand in hand with a more egalitarian distribution of goods and with programs explicitly designed to enlarge the range of what people can do. While such a political perspective does not necessarily require a large government bureaucracy, it is obviously incompatible with a minimal state and complete *laissez faire.*

So while the paradigmatic negative libertarian advocates a society of minimum interference and minimum government, the positive libertarian advocates a society of equality and maximum opportunity. There is a great deal that these visions share, but there is obviously room for sharp disagreement between their supporters. It is these disagreements which have provoked most of the debate about liberty which the present essay joins. My intention is to set out, explain, and defend a particular version of the positive perspective. I will not try to explain or criticize other positive accounts. The negative family of views I take to be the chief competitor of the present account and, even when not under direct examination, it forms the background for this essay. In fact, this essay can be read as an extended argument aimed at persuading the negative libertarian to embrace the positive account. Before explaining the overall structure of that argument, it will be useful to spend a little more time clarifying the terms of the debate.

1. BERLIN'S DISTINCTION

For most readers of political philosophy, Isaiah Berlin's celebrated lecture, "Two Concepts of Liberty," comes immediately to mind when "positive liberty" is mentioned. One of the ways Berlin distinguishes positive from negative liberty corresponds fairly closely to my use of this terminology. The central account of negative liberty is in terms of the absence of interference, direct or indirect, by other persons. At one point Berlin describes the positive program as

. . . the elimination of obstacles to my will, whatever these obstacles may be – the resistance of nature, of my ungoverned passions, of irrational institutions, of the opposing wills or behaviour of others.[1]

So negative liberty is the absence of human interference, and positive liberty is the absence of any obstacles whatever – including institutions. This is a first approximation of the way I understand the distinction. There are, however, some points I would like to amend in Berlin's formulation. First it is, I think, not just obstacles to actions 'I *will*' that limit my freedom, but also obstacles to actions 'I do not will' (and would not will even if that would do some good). This is a point that Berlin himself makes with respect to negative liberty. The relation between *willing* or *wanting* to act on an alternative, and the liberty that alternative affords, will come in for further discussion in Sections 10 and 14.

Second, I do not in general think of the agent's ungoverned passions as an obstacle whose elimination increases liberty. The question of obstacles in some way "internal" to the agent is a difficult one. But it is one on which my own position is not very far removed from that of Berlin's negative libertarian. As will emerge below (especially in Section 9), I am rather cautious in counting "internal obstacles" as limitations of freedom. Finally, obstacles which could not be removed by any human action, I will count as limitations on freedom at one level but not at another. They do restrict what I call "personal freedom," but not "social liberty." (More on this in Chapter V.)

All these are relatively minor points of disagreement about the distinction. Unfortunately, there are other passages in "Two Concepts" and in the comments which introduce *Four Essays on Liberty* that muddy the water a good deal.

In particular, Berlin intends to include the German idealist tradition among the positive libertarians. This leads to an emphasis on self determination. (For Berlin, positive liberty is what one has when to the question "Who is master?" one can answer, "myself." I would take this to be a matter not of liberty of any sort but of the closely related phenomenon of autonomy. Moreover, looking to the idealists, Berlin imports a rationalist notion of autonomy – mastery by the rational or "higher" self. From this point there has been, Berlin thinks, an historical dialectic whose later stages involve coercion in the name of freedom. Leaders force the masses to be free by eliminating "irrational" options which their "lower selves" might otherwise choose. It is not hard to sympathize with Berlin's ringing denunciation of this development.[2]

Since the autonomy characterization of positive liberty is really quite distinct from a characterization in terms of "the absence of all obstacles" and since much of Berlin's essay is taken up with a criticism of the distortions to which rationalistically conceived autonomy conceptions of liberty give rise, it is not surprising that many people have come away from "Two Concepts" not entirely clear as to what the two concepts are.

The situation is further complicated by the fact that Berlin sometimes characterizes negative liberty in a way very close to that in which a positive libertarian, of the sort I have in mind, characterizes positive liberty. The paradigmatic question of negative liberty for Berlin is, "Over what area am I master?" This is equally appropriate, if not more appropriate, for the positive libertarian. Moreover, positive liberty is a matter of "how many doors are open" or are "closed" as the result of "alterable human practices." But these are metaphors Berlin uses to characterize negative liberty. There is, in fact, so much in common between portions of Berlin's account of negative liberty and what I intend by positive liberty, that I will make use of some of Berlin's analytical categories in my characterization of personal freedom in Section 11. Still it should be emphasized that there is more than a shift of labels separating Berlin and the position I will develop. While there are slips here and there, the central theme of Berlin's account of negative liberty really is classically negative. He identifies liberty with the absence of human interference.[3] The welfare mother would count for Berlin as being free to vacation on Corfu, and the opposite view is argued to be a confusion.[4] The substance of that argument will be examined in Sections 21 and 22. For now the important point is that Berlin's distinction between positive and negative liberty does correspond in large part to the way that distinction will be used in this essay. But it must be remembered that the positive liberty I will be defending is a matter of the presence of options and opportunities, not a matter of self mastery or rationality. While the Hegelian account of liberty might count as paradigmatically positive for Berlin, Hegel is not a positive libertarian as I understand that phrase, and as I understand Hegel. There will be only a little contact in what follows with the idealist tradition on liberty.[5] This does not reflect a belief that tradition ought not to be taken seriously. However, it has been the

Anglo-American liberal tradition which has set the context for most of the problems I will explore.

2. MacCallum on positive and negative liberty

The whole idea of distinguishing between positive and negative liberty was challenged in a 1967 paper by Gerald MacCallum.[6] His chief claim is that there are not two different concepts or kinds of freedom because political or social freedom can always be analyzed in terms of a single triadic relation:

[agent] x is (is not) free from y to do (not do, become, not become) z.[7]

Disputes about freedom, according to MacCallum, are not properly understood as disputes about what freedom is, or what "true" or "important" freedom is, but rather about the range of the variables in this relation.

For example, idealists might take x to range over "rational selves," while the rest of us would take the range of x to be persons, more as we ordinarily conceive them. In terms of this schema, the primary difference between the negative and positive accounts of liberty, as I use those terms, is the range of the y variable – the "preventing conditions." The proponent of positive liberty argues for a longer list of preventing conditions as constituting limitations on liberty. For example, poverty typically will not be included among liberty's preventing conditions on the negative account, while it will on the positive.

There is also a difference between the positive account and some negative accounts with respect to the range of the z variable – goal actions or states. Some would say that the deaf person who cannot pay for a hearing-restoring operation is neither free nor unfree to hear a symphony: he or she is simply *incapable* of doing so. I shall say that the deaf person is unfree to hear the symphony, as well as incapable.

So I am in agreement with MacCallum that at least many disputes about liberty can fruitfully be represented as disputes about one or more of his three variables. In fact, a great deal of what follows will be stated in terms of disagreements about preventing conditions.

I am also in agreement with MacCallum that there are not two fundamentally different kinds of freedom. I will devote quite a few pages to the demonstration of the continuity between the positive and negative accounts. It turns out, I think, that the line between positive and negative liberty is, in many important respects, so insubstantial and arbitrary that there is no very good moral reason to insist upon it. This is to say that there is no very good moral reason to insist upon the restricted negative list of preventing conditions.

I am less sure about MacCallum's claim that there are not two different *concepts* of liberty. My uncertainty here is due to the familiar problem that it is hard to know how to count concepts. Those who, like Berlin and MacCallum, want to dispute about the number of concepts owe us some account of their individuation. My suspicion would be that there is either one concept of liberty or else a great many. But I am not sure that talking about concepts is ever productive of clarity.

About two claims I am pretty sure that MacCallum is wrong. The first is that there are not different *kinds* of liberty. Different *fundamental* kinds is one thing, but different kinds is another. If legal liberty has a more restricted set of preventing conditions than social liberty, as it does on nearly all accounts, why not say that legal liberty is one kind of liberty and social another? The kidnap victim is free to escape with respect to legal freedom, since there is no law against escape, while, perhaps, not being free to escape with respect to a broader freedom.

If we take liberty always to be representable by MacCallum's triadic relation then, in extensional terms, just what relation we have, in a given case, will depend upon what we take the ranges of the variables to be. This surely constitutes one perfectly good sense in which there may be different kinds of liberty. Indeed, extensional non-equivalence has impeccable traditional credentials as a criterion of kindhood.

For similar reasons, I have doubts about MacCallum's claims that the disputes ought not to be taken as being "about what *freedom* is"[8] and that freedom is "always one and the same triadic relation."[9] If freedom is a triadic relation, then an argument about the ranges of the three variables is, in the most straightforward sense, an argument about which triadic relation freedom is. Of course, all such relations will have some things in common – though, again extensionally construed, two of them might well have disjoint memberships. Each will draw the first element of each ordered triple from among all those things which anyone (or perhaps any reasonable political philosopher) has taken to be subjects of freedom; each will draw the second and third elements from the similarly widely defined sets of preventing conditions and goal actions. Any freedom relation constructed in this manner is similar to any other, but the similarity relation is a weak one.

So, while agreeing with MacCallum that positive and negative liberty are not two wholly different phenomena, and agreeing as well that the distinction has sometimes produced historical classifications of dubious utility, I shall nonetheless use the distinction, and think of it as dividing liberty into two kinds. The primary principle of division is in terms of the preventing conditions. I shall call "negative" those accounts of personal freedom or social liberty on which the preventing conditions are significantly more restricted than on the account I develop – unless there is no sensible way of fitting the restricted preventing conditions under the "absence of interference" heading.

While dealing with terminological matters, there are two more points that I should mention. First is the question of what to call the possible doings that MacCallum represents with his z variable and Berlin talks about at different times as "the area over which I am master," "possibilities," and "open doors." "Options" and "opportunities" are two additional candidates that I have made provisional use of above. The word I have settled on, however, is "alternatives." It has a little more of the flavor of choice about it than does the austere word "possibilities," while being sufficiently neutral to serve in a wide range of contexts. We can say, for example, that my only alternatives were 'to hand over my money or to have my head blown off.' We cannot say that my only opportunities were 'to hand over my money or to have my head blown off.'

As a final terminological note, I will use "freedom" and "liberty" interchangeably in most contexts, as seems to be the dominant practice. I will exhibit some preference for the combinations "personal freedom" and "social liberty," but I do not attach any significance to this preference.

3. THE STRATEGY OF THE ARGUMENT

I will build up my account of liberty in Chapters II – V, starting out with the conditions which make one free or unfree to perform a particular action, and ending up with an analysis of one's total social liberty, given all the actions one is free to perform. In the course of developing this account, I will find several opportunities to examine and criticize the rival, negative, account.

In the fifth chapter, I will also develop some of the policy implications of a positive account of liberty. Insofar as the sort of society these implications suggest seems attractive, that will itself constitute grounds for adopting the positive account, since it is the most natural and economical account of liberty, given that social ideal. This "policy argument" is chiefly found in Chapter V, though relevant considerations will turn up elsewhere, especially in Chapters VII and VIII.

In Chapter VI, I take up and find wanting some of the chief criticisms that have been leveled against positive accounts of liberty. In particular, I deal with charges that positive accounts are guilty of confusions and linguistic improprieties and are in conflict with deep features of our morality. In defeating the latter charges, I try to show that there is no morally significant difference between the preventing conditions of negative liberty and the wider set of preventing conditions of positive liberty.

This "moral similarity" argument, a second major affirmative argument for the positive account, actually gets started in some of the criticisms of the negative account made in Chapters II and III, where I examine the strains created in trying to keep positive elements out of the negative accounts.

The seventh chapter defends the proposition that liberty, positively understood, is valuable both as a means and as an end. The heart of the argument for the intrinsic value of liberty lies in the link between liberty and autonomy. Considerations of the intrinsic value of liberty confirm and extend the moral similarity argument for the positive account. The structure and scope of positive liberty correspond to the value foundations *better* than do those of negative liberty. This is not because negative liberty is "off" the foundations, but simply because those foundations extend beyond negative liberty.

Some of the costs and limits of liberty are examined in the final chapter, with special attention to the issue of paternalism and conflicts between liberty and democracy.

Let me emphasize that the major arguments that I will develop on behalf of the positive account of liberty are normative arguments. There are "conceptual" or "linguistic" components to some of my arguments, but they are not doing the chief work. I do take up ordinary language objections to positive liberty in Section 23, since a good number of political philosophers have thought such objections to be substantial. On inspection, it will turn out that ordinary language considerations support a positive account of liberty more than they undermine it.

Even where it tends to my advantage, however, I do not want to take ordinary language too seriously. Ordinary language, as well as the semi-technical language of political philosophy, is influenced by ideology – usually the prevailing ideology. If we look to language for answers about politically sensitive questions, we may find some, but they will not necessarily be answers we want to make our own. The interesting questions, in any event, are not about uses of "liberty" or the concept of liberty, but about liberty itself. And the analysis of liberty itself is primarily an exercise in normative theory rather than a conceptual undertaking. Language locates only the general neighborhood in which the phenomenon of liberty is to be found. Its detailed delineation is a matter of what fits best with our political and moral theory and intuitions. So the key issues, in the end, will turn out to be issues of values and social policy.

This is to say that an account of liberty is and ought to be "ideological" in the broad and non-pejorative sense of that word. Berlin's "Two Concepts," for example, reflects a cold war liberalism widely held in British and American academic circles at the time Berlin gave his address.

While I do not share these politics, I do think that Berlin was deporting himself properly in bringing policy arguments to bear on the question of liberty. To attempt a "value neutral" account of liberty is at best only superficially more sensible than to give a "biology neutral" account of fish.

The ideological perspective underlying the present essay might be called "left libertarianism." It owes a good deal to Marx, though not to Marx as officially interpreted in either East or West. The basic idea of left libertarianism is that the liberty of most individuals ought to be increased by diminishing the power concentrated in the hands of a few privileged individuals, whether they be private owners of industry in the West or high ranking bureaucrats in either East or West. I cannot, in this essay, give a full description of left libertarian politics, let alone a full argument for it. However, the positive account of liberty which I will give is itself a sizeable piece of a left libertarian political philosophy. (A large piece that this essay will touch on only very lightly is the role of, and justification for, a radical majoritarian democracy extending into the economy.)

Let me add, as a final introductory note that, while my main purpose is to persuade negative libertarians and to give aid and comfort to those whose prior intuitions have tended along positive lines, I am also concerned to change the mind of the reader who believes, or suspects, that the whole dispute is "merely verbal." The dispute is, of course, in part verbal. It is a matter of how the word "liberty" ought to be used. But considerations relevant to the deployment of this bit of terminology are numerous, and go deep into our moral and political theory. The sense in which we can use "liberty" any way we choose will turn out to be no more interesting than the sense in which we can use "inflation" or "electron" any way we choose.

CHAPTER II

THE FREEDOM TO DO A PARTICULAR
THING: THE OBJECTIVE SIDE

Questions of freedom are of several sorts. One concerns the individual's freedom to do something particular – like speaking in the park on a certain afternoon. Another concerns the individual's "total" freedom – just how free the individual is, considering all the things he or she is and is not free to do. It is this latter question that is relevant to the further question of the freedom, or lack of freedom, of an institution or society.

Since the freedom to do particular things is, presumably, a component, of some sort, in the individual's total freedom, it is natural to start our inquiry by examining the freedom to do particular things. Actually the expression "the freedom to do a *particular* thing" may be slightly misleading, since what we are usually talking about is a class of possible actions fitting under a common description. 'Anabel will give a speech this afternoon in the park' would be made true by any number of different speeches, at different times, in different parts of the park. So 'Anabel is free to speak this afternoon in the park' asserts Anabel's freedom to do any one of many different things. (Even if there is only "one" speech Anabel will be permitted to give, there will always be some possible variation in the way she gives it – at least short of science fiction situations.) So in talking about freedom to do a particular thing, I really intend freedom to do something falling under a description.

My purpose in this chapter and the next is to examine the truth conditions of sentences of the form 'A is free to do x.' In the first place, this involves finding the preventing conditions which ought to be counted as falsifying the freedom claim. I will start with preventing conditions which are uncontroversial, being embraced by even the strictest negative libertarian. I will try to show, however, that the restrictive, negative, set of preventing conditions can be held onto only at considerable cost in terms of the simplicity of the account. I will also show, as against most, though not all, negative views, that freedom to do x is best taken to be a matter of degree. This will arise in the course of an examination of such matters as the costs and probabilities of performing a given action. I will then turn to some vexing issues involving the subjective components of freedom – the relation of freedom to do x to beliefs about x, desires to do x, and psychological barriers to doing x. After having won, from all this, a fairly good idea what it is for *A* to be free to degree *d* to do *x*, we can then go on to consider '*A* is free to degree *d*.'

4. RESTRAINT AND INCAPACITY

Since a positive account of liberty incorporates and extends the basic ideas of the negative account, especially with respect to preventing conditions, and since it does this over the strenuous objections of negative accounts, it will be useful to use negative accounts as a starting point.

Traces of the negative account of liberty have been found as far back as Aristotle. But it was its clear and forceful formulation by Hobbes that established its central place in British political philosophy. Hobbes's characterization explicitly rejects the positive preventing condition of incapacity due to sickness.

Liberty, or freedom, signifieth, properly, the absence of opposition: by opposition, I mean external impediments of motion; . . . whatsoever is so tied, or environed, as it cannot move but within a certain space, which space is determined by the opposition of some external body, we say it hath no liberty to go further . . . But when the impediment of motion is in the constitution of the being itself, we use not to say it wants the liberty, but the *power* to move; as when a stone lieth still, or a man is fastened to his bed by sickness. And according to the proper and generally received meaning of the word, *a "freeman" is he that in those things which by his strength and wit he is able to do, is not hindered to do what he has a will to do.*[1]

Understanding "opposition" and "hindrance" in terms of physical restraint, as we are instructed, it should be clear that this is a very strict account of unfreedom indeed. In short, it is a chains and walls account. Not even coercion counts as a hindrance which makes an action unfree in this, Hobbes's primary, sense.

Fear and liberty are consistent; as when a man throweth his goods into the sea for *fear* the ship should sink, he doth it nevertheless very willingly, and may refuse to do it if he will; it is therefore the action of one that was *free*: so a man sometimes pays his debt, only for fear of imprisonment, . . . And generally all actions which men do in commonwealths, for fear of the law, are actions which the doers had liberty to omit.[2]

This liberty, for which not even the threat of the gallows is a preventing condition, Hobbes called "corporal liberty." It was not the only kind of liberty Hobbes was interested in. In fact, he was largely concerned with the "liberty of the subject" which is roughly what we would call "legal liberty." But corporal liberty is of interest for present purposes because of its reliance on the preventing condition of physical restraint. We might call it "liberty as the absence of restraint." However, Hobbes' "corporal liberty" is itself not quite as strict in one respect as a typical negative account of non-restraint. If Bernice, who is strong and healthy, is buried by an avalanche, she would be corporally unfree to walk to the warming hut. But since Bernice is not restrained as the result of the direct actions of another person, a strict negative account will not take her to be unfree.

The feature I wish to examine now, however, is common to both official negative non-restraint and Hobbesian corporal freedom. It is a notion of restraint strictly distinguished from such incapacities as those brought on by illness. The crucial question for the positive-negative debate is whether an account of liberty can be worked out in detail, which includes restraint, but not incapacity among its preventing conditions.

We are not to say, I take it, that someone is restrained by a staircase from getting to the library, simply because that person is too sick to climb the stairs. This is a case of incapacity, not restraint. Other people could climb the stairs. On the other hand, I am, I take it, restrained by a set of chains, even if some people – namely, world class weightlifters – could break out of them. I am even restrained by chains which *I* could break out of if I had trained long and hard for such feats of strength. Moreover, I am restrained, I would think, when tied up with a cord which I could break if I were well, but, as the perpetrator of the deed knows, I am not strong enough to break since I am sick.

One might be tempted to think that A is restrained by a device W (chain, wall, or what-have-you) from doing x if and only if:

(1) A cannot surmount W and as a result cannot do x, and
(2) If A's inability to surmount W is the result of some special incapacity or disability of A's, then W was deployed by some person B who believes that A cannot surmount W and who intends to restrain A.

Ignore, for now, any problems lurking under "as a result," "cannot," and "special incapacity." The formulation seems headed into immediate problems by requiring that B believe that W will restrain and that B intend to restrain.

Suppose that Clarissa jokingly handcuffs Delbert to a statue of Genghis Khan in the parlor. Under normal circumstances, the trick to opening the handcuffs is literally child's play to figure out. Delbert could do it easily, as Clarissa knows. Unhappily, shortly after the handcuffs were applied, a fire breaks out. In their panic, everyone forgets about Delbert, who in his panic (a problem he is specially liable to) cannot extricate himself from the handcuffs. There follows the inevitable tragic consequence. Surely, for Hobbes and the negative tradition, as well as the rest of us, Delbert was restrained from leaving the house, despite the fact that Clarissa neither intended to restrain him nor believed that he would be restrained.

There is something of a puzzle here, because Delbert's panic-induced incapacity to get out of toy handcuffs seems different from a panic-induced inability to find one's way out of the house. Wandering around in the house, when there is a reasonably simple way out, Delbert is not restrained, however unable he may be to get out. Manacled by toy cuffs, he is restrained, however easy it would be for a normal person to get out of them.

However, this puzzle is not hard to solve. Certain devices, including ropes, chains, handcuffs, locks, walls, and moats, are paradigmatic re-straining devices. When they prevent somebody from doing something by operating in the classic way or some reasonable facsimile, it counts as restraint, even if they are old, generally ineffective, or toys. This remains true even if the device is only effective because of some special incapacity of the victim. A heavy rope, accidentally left across a sick person's chest, may not count as a restraint – for the fastidious. But when that rope is tied, however poorly and with whatever intentions and beliefs, it becomes a restraint – if it cannot be untied by the victim.

Other sorts of barriers must meet somewhat higher standards to count as restraint, at least for the negative tradition. A heavy suitcase acciden-tally left in front of the sick-room door will not be a restraint on the negative account, even if it proves an insurmountable barrier for the sick person. However, I would think that the same suitcase placed with the intention of restraining, and the knowledge that it will work, does restrain on the negative account. This all suggests the following unlovely formula-tion. A is restrained by W from doing x if and only if:

(1) a cannot surmount W and as a result cannot do x, and
(2) Either (a) W was deployed by someone who believes that A will not be able to surmount W and who intends thus to restrain A, (b) W is or essentially involves a classical restraining device (or something similar) used in the standard way.

This is probably still not quite right as an explication of restraint for the negative tradition. Suppose A is recovering from a weakening illness. B puts a book on a high shelf, believing that A will want the book badly enough to expend the considerable energy necessary to retrieve it. Succeeding in doing so, B believes, will raise A's spirits and belief in recovery. In fact, however, B has miscalculated. A tries to retrieve the book but is still too weak. I would think that (what turns out to be) the inaccessible height of the book, restrains A from getting it, even though B did not believe that it would.

This suggests amending clause (2a) as follows: W was deployed by someone who believed that A will have at least some difficulty in surmounting W. But this still seems wrong in requiring that B have had A in mind at all in setting out W. B may have been trying to restrain someone else, or simply whoever happened to come along. (Fences are not usually put up to stop someone in particular.) So some modification along these lines is needed in our formulation.

Just how this modification ought to be made is unclear to me, however, because I am unsure about such cases as the following: Suppose B sets up a nursery fence to keep a two year old out of the kitchen. Suffering from an attack of dizziness, A is not able to get over the fence. Is A restrained and hence unfree to go into the kitchen, or is A simply incapable of going into the kitchen?

This all suggests that it is going to be difficult to distinguish between restraint and incapacity and that any such distinction will have a considerable element of arbitrariness. If this is so, we may be buying trouble if we insist, with the negative tradition, that restraints, but not incapacities, make people unfree.

Consider, for example, the following case. I unload you onto an isolated island with no means of escape. Surely by forcibly putting you in a situation where natural barriers prevent you from doing x, I have restrained you from doing x. (A prison made from a natural cave is no less a prison.) In this case you are, among other things, restrained from going to Walla Walla. Presumably you are still restrained, on the negative account, the next day, the next year and to the end of your life. Peculiarly, it would seem as if the people *born* on an equally isolated island, with no means of escape, are not restrained (in the key sense) from going to Walla Walla. (Suppose they even want to, as the result of a tourist brochure which washed ashore.) They are not restrained because no human agency interfered to put them in their predicament. So they are simply incapable of getting to Walla Walla, not unfree to do so.

This seems odd enough, but what are we to say about the descendants of the forcible exiles born on our first desert island? Does birth wipe clean the slate? Will there be a time when half of the population on the island is restrained and hence unfree to go to Walla Walla, while the other half is free but incapable – though everyone can do exactly the same things? Or is the moral character of the original forcible act of exile somehow transmitted down from one generation to another (even if long forgotten), so that the descendants of the exiles remain restrained until they can get off the island? (And what if one is descended from both exiles and natives?)

This is, I think, just the beginning of the potentially embarrassing questions which can be asked of the negative account's restraint-incapacity distinction. Let me suggest a few more. Is A made unfree by intentionally limiting A's capacities through the use of drugs, undernourishment, sleep deprivation, amputation, and the like? (If so, the forced amputee, for example, will be unfree to do things that the naturally limbless are not unfree to do.) Do I ever make A unfree to do x by making it more painful for A to do x? If so, how are the variations in pain thresholds or tolerance to be worked into the account? Is a lower threshold an incapacity? (A very *high* threshold, especially complete insensitivity to pain, is usually counted an incapacity.)

I hope this all makes it plausible that tying freedom and unfreedom to the distinction between incapacity and restraint, threatens paradox. At the very least, those who are committed to the negative account of freedom owe us a characterization of the restraint-incapacity distinction which is reasonably intuitive, not horribly complex, and avoids these difficulties.

The last question above, about using pain as a restraint, involves a whole new set of issues as well as those of restraint and incapacity. Preventing A from doing x by raising A's (expected) cost in doing x constitutes a broad family of restraint distinct from strict physical restraint or "corporal unfreedom." While some of these issues arise in contexts where the costs make the agent unfree without coercing the agent, little will be lost by considering them in the special but important case of coercion.

5. COERCION

After strict physical restraint and strict physical compulsion (which is just "restraint in motion" as when A pushes B through the window), the next most important of the traditional negative preventing conditions is coercion. Understanding when A is unfree to do x by virtue of coercion is a large step towards the analysis of 'A is free to do x.' It is also a step, as it turns out, that will require altering our intended destination slightly. The analysis will become that of 'A is free to degree d to do x.'

If we are to believe the *Oxford English Dictionary*, ordinary English employs "coercion" in quite a broad sense: "constraint, restraint, compulsion; the application of force to control the action of a voluntary agent." Philosophers, however, have tended to use "coercion" more narrowly, concentrating centrally, if not exclusively, on cases where the action of an agent is controlled by threatening the agent. For the most part, I will follow this general tendency. "Restraint" and "compulsion" can cover most of the territory left uncovered by this restricted use of "coercion."

However, I think it would be unintuitive to follow some recent treatments[3] in restricting "coercion" to cases where there are explicit or implicit threats or threatening offers.[4] In the first place, certain situations are coercive in which the coercer does not threaten, but arranges things so that undesired consequences will automatically befall the agent if the agent does not do what the coercer wishes.

For example, I throw one life jacket to a pair of drowning swimmers who are in danger far too immediate for them to work out any rational procedure for deciding who gets the preserver. My intention is to force them to fight over the preserver. If I succeed, I would think that I have coerced them into fighting. I do not threaten an evil consequence, though an evil consequence does threaten, so to speak, and I make use of that fact. As in many cases of coercion, a great deal here depends upon the intentions of the coercer. If I had but one life preserver to throw, and did so with the innocent hope that at least one victim will be saved, then I would not have coerced the victims into their fight.

Another sort of case which departs from paradigmatic coercion occurs when the intent to coerce is absent. Consider Nozick's example of the foreigner who, in an attempt to be friendly, exercises his one sentence of English – a sentence he does not understand. He carefully pronounces "Your money or your life," while exhibiting his knife for his neighbor at the bar to admire. The neighbor turns over his money.[5]

There is some temptation to say that the neighbor was coerced into turning over his money. There is less temptation to say that the foreigner coerced him into doing so. On the one side, what was uttered is typically a threat, and the neighbor had the best sorts of reason to think it was a threat. Suppose we are concerned with the neighbor's freedom and his responsibility in the loss of the money. From this point of view, the situation was functionally equivalent to a paradigmatic case of coercion. The neighbor ought to behave in exactly the same way he would if the threat were intended. The excuse he can make for having parted with the money is no less strong than it would be had the threat been real. It is natural, then, to assimilate this case to the phenomenon of coercion.

On the other hand, there are at least two policy considerations which ought to lead us to be hesitant in using "coercion" in unintended threat cases. In the first place, we don't want to allow the coercion excuse to be used too widely. Nearly anything one says or does can be mistaken for a coercive threat by someone sufficiently deranged or misinformed. In some cases where people think they are coerced, they are not. But in the present case, anyone who is reasonably prudent would think that he or she had been threatened. So a concern to protect the force of the coercion excuse does not require us to exclude this case.

The second reason we may be hesitant to cry "coercion" in unintended threat cases is that our concerns about coercion extend beyond the purported victim and his or her responsibility, excuses, and freedom.

Private coercion is often illegal, and frequently immoral even when it is not illegal. A society has a legitimate interest in limiting coercion. This interest focuses attention on the potential coercer and how to prevent him or her from coercing. From this point of view, the only kinds of unintended threats that interest us are those which arise through something like negligence. In other cases, we do not want to saddle the unintentional threatener with the title, "coercer." Now our foreigner was, perhaps, a little less than fully prudent, both in exhibiting a knife when he could not communicate unambiguously, and in speaking a sentence whose meaning he did not know. Still, the likelihood that these actions would lead to harm was probably low enough.

For these sorts of reasons, we are reluctant to say that the foreigner coerced his neighbor. And then, of course, it becomes odd to say that the neighbor was coerced. My suspicion, however, is that neither ordinary language nor our policy considerations really settle the issue. Perhaps it is best simply to say that there is a strict use of "coercion" which requires the intent[6] to influence behavior – usually through a threat. On a less strict use, someone who has good grounds for believing that he or she has been so threatened, may be said to have been coerced.

There is also, it seems to me, a perfectly well understood use of "coercion" in which non-human conditions may coerce. Rising water may coerce the fugitive out of the cave, whether it is a result of a sudden downpour or the deliberate action of the fire department. It is not at all clear to me whether this is an "ordinary" use, an "extended" use, or perhaps even a "metaphorical" use of "coercion." In any event, such cases will not play any role in my arguments.

Let me shift consideration now to a more nearly standard case of coercion. Suppose that your employer threatens to fire you if you join a union. You can join a union under these circumstances, but the cost will be high. If, in view of the threat, your prior reasons for wanting to join the union recede to relative insignificance and you do not join, then you were coerced.

A wide range of states of affairs can be threatened coercively. Some of them are not bad in isolation. For example, Esmeralda threatens to set Farnsworth's inheritance at $10,000. Farnsworth, of course, will be glad to get the $10,000. Still, this constitutes a threat if Esmeralda's will previously named Farnsworth as a $100,000 beneficiary. (Notice that it is a coercive threat independently of whether Farnsworth had any *right* to the $100,000.) So one may coerce A simply by threatening to lower A's prospects, whatever those prospects were based on. One can also coerce A by threatening to lower the prospects of persons A cares about, or by threatening to damage things A cares about.

But if a wide range of threats can be used coercively, obviously not all threats are coercive in all contexts. A great deal depends upon the seriousness of the harm threatened and the significance of the action one is to be coerced into doing (or not doing). A threatened punch in the nose might be enough to coerce me into buying a beer for a member of a street gang. The same threat would not be sufficient to coerce me into robbing a bank. In making this last claim, I do not mean simply that I wouldn't rob a bank if so threatened. I mean also that, if I did rob a bank, I would not be able to plead that I had been coerced into so doing by a threatened punch in the nose.

The situation is complicated by the fact that coercion is a matter of probabilities as well as costs. The most important probablistic element is the credibility of the threat. Frequently we suspect that a threat may be a bluff – the threatener being, in fact, unwilling or unable to carry out the threat. The credibility of threats comes in all degrees. At one extreme there is the bravado of 'I'll demolish you,' addressed by a small second grader to the playground bully. At the other extreme is the utterly convincing threat of the concentration camp guard to beat anyone who steps out of line.

The degree of credibility a threat must have to be coercive varies with two variables already mentioned – the seriousness of the harm threatened and the significance of the target action. A threat to blow my head off need not be quite as believable to be coercive, as a threat not to deliver my newspaper. At least part of the lower credibility required of high stake threats is explained in terms of the standard-expected-utility theory. (Multiply the probability of an outcome by its net gain or loss.) In particular, it is easy to see why low credibility bomb threats are often taken seriously.

The relevant notion of probability would seem to depend largely upon the beliefs of the person coerced, just as the relevant notion of costs depends largely upon the values of the person coerced. But there is need for caution here, because we would not want to say that someone was coerced into robbing a bank by a threatened punch in the nose, even if that person had a very strong aversion to being punched in the nose and a relatively mild aversion to bank robbery. Similarly, we would not usually want to count someone as coerced by the threat of a seven year old to blow up the world, even if the person took the threat seriously. Perhaps these cases are to be handled, in part, by a restriction of the relevant values and beliefs to "reasonable" ones. If we have to explain behavior in terms of lunacy anyway, there is little need to explain it in terms of coercion. I will take a more detailed look at probabilities and beliefs in Sections 7 and 8.

Setting aside the dubious and difficult area of the irrational coerced agent, it might seem as if the phenomenon of coercion could be understood entirely in terms of expected utilities. Suppose I come home to find an unarmed robber ransacking my belongings. Upon seeing me, the robber grabs a prominently placed oil painting. He threatens to tear it up unless I give him my money and let him escape.

Am I coerced by this threat? Well, suppose that I estimate the credibility of the threat at .8. (The robber is in a desperate position and has the look of a painting ripper. On the other hand, he stands to gain nothing by carrying out the threat and might possibly be hit with a harsher sentence or a larger restitution bill if caught. Perhaps it is a clever bluff.) Having settled on my credibility figure, I ought to hand over my money if and only if the amount of money I have is less than .8 times the value in dollars I place on the painting. If I have more money than that, it is irrational for me to hand it over. If I do hand it over, under these circumstances, it is doubtful that I can reasonably claim that I was coerced into doing so.

In this case, then, there is no vagueness in the notion of coercion. Once I have settled on a degree of credibility for the threat, and a value for the painting, the rest is arithmetic. A sub-coercive threat should have no effect on my behavior, and would not limit my freedom.

If this were true in every case (at least involving rational agents), it would have the interesting consequence that coercion would be an "all or nothing" phenomenon rather than a matter of degree. This would fit especially well with the way the negative account has traditionally understood coercion in particular and unfreedom in general. So, does the generalization of the above reasoning work?

Let P be the expected utility to A of doing the action x. Let R be the expected utility to A of refraining from doing x in the absence of B's threat. Let R' be the expected utility of refraining from doing x in the presence of B's threat. Here, then, are the principles suggested by the above case.

(1) If $P > R$, B does not coerce A into doing x.
(2) If $P \leq R'$, B does not coerce A into doing x.
(3) If $R \geq P \geq R'$, B does coerce A into doing x.

If these principles were correct, and making the rather large assumption that we could quantify all costs and benefits involved, we would get crisp dividing lines between coercive and non-coercive threats. How do (1) – (3) fare upon examination? To start on a positive note, (2) is clearly correct – assuming rationality on A's part. If refraining from doing x has a higher expected utility than doing x, even given the coercive threat, then the threat ought to be ineffective. Either the harm threatened is not severe enough, or the credibility of the threat is too low.

Unfortunately for the possibility of giving a simple account of coercion, principles (1) and (3) are not as successful as (2). (1) is wrong because I can be coerced into doing a thing I would have done anyway. (Just as I can be restrained from leaving a place where I have chosen to stay.) If someone forces me to walk to lunch with a gun at my head, I am coerced. This is so even if I had already chosen to go to lunch and would be doing little different if the gun were not at my head. In the one case I could have changed my mind and skipped lunch; in the other I could not. It is that fact that reveals the difference.

Of course, B's threat is not always coercive where A was already planning to do x anyway, even if A pays some attention to the threat. If the reasons A already had for doing x are much weightier than those introduced by B's threat, then A is not coerced.

We could get closer to the truth by replacing (1) with this principle:

(1') If $P > R$, then A is coerced into doing x if and only if $R - R' > P - R$.

Roughly, this says that the threat-introduced reasons to do x must be greater than the pre-existing net reasons for preferring x. But this is still too crude, as we shall see.

Principle (3) is also wrong. It asserts that a threat is coercive if it tips the utility balance relevant to the decision. But suppose that I am trying to decide whether or not to take a trip to Borneo. There are many weighty reasons for making the trip, but also many weighty considerations on the other side. The two are roughly in balance. Knowing I am contemplating a trip, believing I am fanatically attached to my begonias, and hoping to coerce me into staying, you threaten not to water my begonias if I go. Now, in fact, my attachment to my begonias is far less than you believe, but I would somewhat prefer that they survive. So I add your rather lightweight threat to my reasons for staying home, and conclude that they are now marginally more telling than the considerations on the other side. As a result, I decide not to make the trip. You intended to coerce me by significantly lowering my prospects if I went. Your threat was effective in keeping me from going. But it was just one minor consideration which happened to tip the scales of the decision. Your threat did not "force" my decision.

Obviously this case discredits (1') as well as (3). (1') is more liberal than (3) in counting a situation as coercive, even where the threat does not tip the balance – so long as the change it introduces in the expected utilities is greater than the prior net expected utility of the favored choice, and provided as well that the threat favors the same choice. Clearly a begonia case applies here too, since I might already have decided to stay home – as the result of a very slight difference between very weighty considerations. That the begonia threat was weightier than these net prior reasons still would not make it coercive.

In short, whether a threat is serious enough to count as coercive depends not just on "net" considerations, derived from subtracting one set of expected utilities from another, but on "ratio" considerations of the relative weightiness of the threat as against the other reasons for acting and refraining already in the field. While "net" considerations might give us crisp dividing lines between cases of coercion and non-coercion, the sort of ratio considerations we have been driven to will not. We will be stuck with such formulations as "the threat must be considerably weightier than the other reasons" or "if the other reasons pro and con are very weighty, then the threat must have at least a respectable fraction of their weight."

The reason the threatened painting-ripping case turned out so neatly can now be seen to be a result of the fact that I tacitly assumed that I had no reasons of significant weight for handing over the money or refraining from doing so, except the value of the money and the value of the painting. There being no additional significant considerations either way, "percentage weight" was not involved.

So, except in special simple cases, an "all or nothing" notion of coercion risks serious vagueness. We could eliminate the vagueness in particular cases by adopting a cut-off point by convention. (To do so in general would require a more uniform means of quantifying utilities across cases than we are likely to come up with.) But any such conventional line separating coercive threats from sub-coercive threats (with their relatively lower credibility or seriousness of harm threatened) would have to be arbitrary. This is fatal to an "all or nothing" notion of coercion for purposes of an account of liberty, since the weakest coercive threat will be morally very similar to the strongest subcoercive threat. The sub-coercive threat will be only slightly less compelling and should be only slightly less a limitation of liberty. The conclusion I draw is that coercion is a matter of degree. Pretty obviously, this same conclusion applies to restraints which operate by raising costs (rather than by creating outright impossibilities). It follows, then, that the freedom to do x will itself be a matter of degree in at least those cases where coercive and cost-restraintive preventing conditions are involved.

Now typically the negative tradition has treated A's freedom to do x as if it were not a matter of degree.[7] Either someone interferes to prevent A's doing x, or no one does. But there is nothing incoherent about a negative account's accepting degrees of restraint, coercion, interference and, thereby, degrees of freedom to do x. But employing degrees of freedom to do x nearly requires that the account accept degrees of liberty when it comes to the individual's total freedom. And this does pose problems for the negative account, as we shall see in Section 10.

6. COERCION AND THE WAGE AGREEMENT

I want now to take a brief sidetrip from the main line of argument to consider a controversial question of political economy involving coercion. In so doing, I will try to avoid using anything in the preceding section with which the negative libertarian might disagree. Using relatively un-controversial premises, I want to show that it is incorrect for negative libertarians to deny the possibility that workers in a "free enterprise" market economy are coerced, by the "proper" workings of that system, into accepting the terms of their employment.

Consider first what I hope will seem a clear case of coercion. Gideon owns the town hardware store and sells, among other things, fire fighting equipment designed for the small property owner. A serious brush fire breaks out in the community, threatening many homes. Gideon responds to the increased demand by increasing the price ten-fold on anything which might be useful in fighting fires. He succeeds in nearly balancing supply and demand, and his stock is bought out in an orderly manner. There is, however, a certain amount of ill-feeling against Gideon. The home owners believe that they were coerced into paying the extra money.

In his defense, Gideon points out that he did not start the fire. He even helped fight it himself. Moreover, he did not withhold fire fighting equipment. All of his equipment was sold, and only slightly less quickly than it would have been at its ordinary price. Gideon, let us suppose, can also truthfully say that it was not his intention to take advantage of anyone. He simply holds a principled belief, formed in economics class in college, that the economy is best served when supply and demand are left to settle prices on their own. Gideon concludes his defense by saying that he did absolutely nothing to force people to buy his equipment.

I take it that all but the most extreme of free enterprisers would reject Gideon's plea that he did not coerce his customers into paying the higher price. Gideon's coercive threat is simply the threat not to sell the equipment unless the new, higher, price is paid. This is a threat and coercive because the moral expectation is that one does not seek a windfall profit at the expense of potential victims of catastrophe. Simi-larly, as Nozick argues, it is usually a coercive threat if one "offers" to rescue a drowning swimmer in exchange for a thousand dollars.[8] In the morally expected course of events, one simply aids people in such situations (assuming there is no great risk to oneself). And in the morally expected course of events in a fire emergency, one either gives away one's stock of fire fighting equipment or, at worst, sells it at the normal price. For A to propose to act contrary to this morally expected course in a way detrimental to B, unless B gives A some special consideration, is for A to threaten B coercively. It is as if A, instead of pointing a gun at B's head, makes use of the fact that the contingencies of the situation have pointed a gun at B's head.

The relatively little disagreement I would expect about the fire equipment case is due to the near universal acceptance of the special moral status of emergency situations. This status, among other things, morally precludes most forms of profiteering.

Now to the controversial issue – the wage agreement. Assume that there is a class of people in a given society who are strictly dependent on employment for survival. They cannot live off the land or sea because it is either all owned or requires equipment or licenses they cannot afford. There is no welfare system – at least for the able-bodied. Under these circumstances will a wage offer determined by the unfettered workings of supply and demand ever be coercive?

If the labor pool is small, demand for labor brisk and competitive, and wages therefore high, there would be little temptation to call the wage agreement coercive. Similarly, before the fire, there were no obvious grounds for calling Gideon's sale of fire equipment (at reasonable prices) coercive.

Suppose now that the labor pool is relatively quite large. As a result employers, without collusion, make lower and lower wage offers. Finally wages sink to the subsistence level. (A little imagination will turn up any number of sets of conditions under which this would actually happen.) The individual is faced with the option of accepting one or another low wage offer or starving.

The Employers' Association points out, correctly let us suppose, that it did not bring about the oversupply of labor. In fact, the employers have contributed to birth control campaigns and followed policies which, as they understand things, ought to stimulate employment. They have no wish to take advantage of anyone, and share Gideon's faith in the beneficence of the unfettered market. They remind us that a worker is always free to refuse a wage offer and to work for someone else. So why say they have coerced their workers?

Most of the defenses of the Employers' Association are obviously parallel to Gideon's defenses. One difference between the two cases is that Gideon could not point to other local sources of fire fighting equipment. But surely the situation would have been morally no different if there were three hardware store owners, all of whom raised their prices so as to approximately balance supply and demand in the fire emergency. One might, then, say that it was the collective action of all three store owners that coerced all the customers, rather than saying that each owner coerced his or her own customers. But this is only a detail. In any event, the existence of the other store owners would not lessen the coerciveness of Gideon's actions. So the parallel between the two cases holds up. The workers may reasonably see the wage offer just as Gideon's customers do his offer to sell. They might as well have guns at their heads. If they do not accept one of the (equally low) wage offers, they will die.

One reason some may believe that there is no coercion here is that they do not perceive the situation as falling under the same category as does the fire emergency. So special moral principles do not come into play. In particular, the employers are under no obligation not to profit as much as they are able from the situation. It does not, it is true, *look* like an emergency unless people start to exercise the option of starving to death. The threat is less apparent than that posed by a raging fire coming ever closer to people's homes. In the one case we see the threat tangible and menacing. In the other we see only a community going about its business; perhaps with some grumbling.

If this explains why some feel that the moral situation differs in the case of demanding the market price for emergency goods and the case of paying the market wage in a labor glut, it does not, yet, justify treating the cases differently. The duties we owe those who are in danger of starving to death are surely at least as demanding as the duties we owe those who are in danger of having their homes burned. The moral strictures against profiteering in fire equipment apply equally against profiteering in a labor glut. Threatening not to employ workers at all except at a subsistence wage is then to threaten to depart from the morally expected course of events to the workers' detriment, and so coerces the workers. In this case, the employers have no *right* to offer the workers nothing more than a subsistence wage.[9]

One further difference between Gideon and the Employers' Association might be brought up at this point. In Gideon's case, I assumed that there was an established normal price for the fire equipment. The coercive situation was brought on by raising the price significantly beyond that normal price. But there may not be any normal price for labor, beyond what the market sets, unless something like a labor theory of value is correct. It might then be objected that, since we cannot specify the wage level that is "morally expected," we cannot charge the employers with being coercive when they take advantage of a low market price.

I think this objection is mistaken, however, because the existence of an established price for the fire equipment is not an essential part of that case. Suppose that the fire equipment is a new addition to Gideon's line.

Market price is not yet established. Still, when the fire emergency strikes, Gideon is not morally permitted to charge whatever the market will bear. At the very least, he is required to sell the equipment close to his own cost if a higher price would make purchase impossible for customers in desperate need of the equipment. Even if all customers could pay higher prices, Gideon would not be morally permitted to go significantly beyond "normal profits." The existence of morally inadmissible profiteering does not require the specification of any exact non-arbitrary line on either profits or prices.

If the employers are doing very poorly, even given the subsistence wages, the wage agreement may not be coercive, but if they are doing very well, then the agreement, under the above conditions, will be coercive.

I admit that I have set an extreme case in making starvation the only alternative to employment, and by setting the market wage at subsistence. It is, however, a case which arose in the nineteenth century and still occurs in some countries today, including advanced ones. But the point of my argument will extend to less extreme cases. After all, a threat of death is not the only thing which brings emergency morality into play, otherwise the threatened loss of a home would be insufficient. Consider being dependent on a miserly and degrading welfare system or having to seek employment which seriously underutilizes your skills and abilities. These are serious enough dislocations of one's life that, when they impend, that fact generates the same moral constraints as does a natural emergency. In particular, no one is permitted to exploit the possibility of such major worsenings of life prospects, by striking the best possible bargain with the individual in question. To do so is coercive. From this perspective, it seems that coercive wage agreements are fairly common features of "free enterprise" economies, especially, though not exclusively, during relatively hard times. So one does not have to go beyond the traditional negative category of coercion to find practices which would be condemned in the name of liberty but which the negative tradition, in its "free enterprise" form, has tended to sanction either from a distance or directly and in detail.

7. THE PROBABILITY OF DOING x

Probability has already come in for some attention in the form of the credibility of a coercive threat. I would now like to take a more detailed look at the relation of probability to being free to do x. In particular, I want to examine cases where there is a probability of less than 1 that A will succeed in doing x if A tries to do x.

Having seen above the necessity of taking freedom to be a matter of degree in coercion and other "perceived cost" cases, it is natural to generalize the account to probabilistic actions, letting the degree of freedom to do x vary with the probability of doing x. Thus, for example, I am only "moderately free" to climb Mt. McKinley since, although there is a fairly good chance that I would succeed in climbing McKinley if I attempted one of the easier routes with a good group, there would also be a significant risk of failure.

Of course, 'I am moderately free to climb McKinley' is not the sort of thing one hears in everyday conversation. One reason it may sound a little odd is that in such contexts we are often concerned with legal freedom, which is not a matter of degree. Legally I am simply free to climb McKinley.

A different explanation of the oddness of 'I am moderately free to climb McKinley' is that we usually understand 'I am free to climb McKinley' as equivalent to 'I am free to attempt to climb McKinley.' The attempt, it might be argued, is not probabilistic, though what it is an attempt at is. Consider the following two hypotheses:

(1) 'A is free to do x' is equivalent to 'A is free to attempt to do x'.
(2) If A chooses to attempt to do x, then A attempts to do x (with probability 1).

If (1) and (2) were correct, we could get away without introducing degrees of freedom except in those cases discussed last section. This would avoid the unintuitive course of saying that I am only very free to walk through my office doorway. (Given the vicissitudes of all flesh, the probability is slightly less than 1 that I will make it through the doorway if I try.)

As it happens, however, both (1) and (2) are false. It is not wholly implausible that 'I am free to climb McKinley' really means 'I am free to attempt to climb McKinley.' But it is wholly implausible that 'I am free to walk through the doorway' really means 'I am free to attempt to walk through the doorway.' The latter could be true if the doorway is booby trapped with explosives, or even if I know the door to be shut and locked.

As for (2), it is, I think, never true that the probability is 1 that one will succeed at *attempting* something. An attempt to do x must always involve some action in addition to the decision to do x. At the very least, there must be a "movement of will." But, given the vicissitudes of all flesh again, something may intervene to prevent any action, even a movement of will. So if we were to take the artificial step of recasting all freedom locutions in terms of attempts, we still would not escape probabilities less than 1. And with that would reappear the attractiveness of taking the freedom to do a particular thing to be a matter of degree.

My proposal is to say that, strictly speaking, one is never absolutely free to do anything.[10] However, when one is very free, in that the probability is very close to 1 that one would succeed, there is no harm in expressing this slightly loosely by saying, for example, that I am free to walk through my office doorway.

Similarly when we have a very low non-zero probability, it is tempting, and usually harmless, to say that A is unfree to do x. Suppose, for example, that I am held by kidnappers who threaten to shoot me if I try to escape. There are several of them with guns, and I know them to be good shots. Still, there is some small probability that they will all miss if I make a quick dive through the window and run for the woods. Since the probability of my succeeding is so low, it is very unattractive to say that I am *free* to leave.

On the other hand, it is also a little embarrassing to say that I was *unfree* to jump through the window and run into the woods if I, in fact, succeed in doing so despite the odds. There is a tendency to think of 'A is unfree to do x' as entailing 'A does not do x.' It should be recalled, however, that 'A is legally unfree to do x' does not entail 'A does not do x.' We might call unfreedom under which A's unfreedom to do x entails that A does not do x, a "decisive" unfreedom. "Physical unfreedom," "logical unfreedom," and "metaphysical unfreedom" (if there is such a thing) would then be decisive. Moral unfreedom, understood as what is not morally permitted, would be non-decisive.

It is a question of some interest just how the various other species of freedom divide up with respect to decisiveness. But there would probably be general agreement among positive as well as negative libertarians that the key sorts of social unfreedom are decisive – including the unfreedom of the above example.

Bearing this in mind, we might try a third account of my freedom to run off into the woods: I am free to run off if and only if I succeed in doing so. This, however, has the unintuitive consequence that two people in exactly the same current situation might one be free and the other not free to run off into the woods. Moreover, I would not always know myself whether I was free or unfree to run off into the woods. And, finally, the kidnappers could object to being indicted, in a case where the victim escapes, since their actions did not render the victim unfree to leave.

My proposal, again, is to take the victim's freedom to be a matter of degree. In this case, the degree of freedom is low, since there is little probability of a successful escape. This approach does seem to fit the facts of the situation. After all, it is a qualitatively different case when the victim is securely restrained. (In that case, the probability of running off into the woods would be 0, and the victim would be strictly unfree to so so.) The degree of freedom account does not become awkward, in our original case, if the victim does escape. However it is, again, easy to understand why, for most practical purposes, we tend to call *very* low degrees of freedom "unfreedom."

An account on which freedom is a matter of degree varying with probability does have some problems, however. First, there is, again, the question of just what approach to probability is appropriate. This matter has come in for some attention above in the special case of the credibility of a threat. The general issue is how far we ought to take as correct the agent's own estimate of his or her chances of succeeding at doing *x*. In coercive situations, the agent's estimate seems to be the crucial probability, so long as it is reasonable on the evidence. But if we are, in general, less free to climb more difficult mountains, there is some reason to think that the real degree of difficulty of the mountain is at least as relevant as the agent's estimate of that difficulty. One might even want to say that the agent's *real* degree of freedom depends wholly on the actual degree of difficulty and only the agent's beliefs about his or her freedom depend upon the agent's own estimates of probability.

There is more reason to emphasize the agent's subjective probability, rather than the objective probability, when coercion is involved. For example, we do not want to shift responsibility from the robber to the teller when the gun turns out to be a realistic looking toy. That is, we do not want to count the teller as having been (very) free not to turn over the money, despite the high objective probability of successfully doing so. On the other hand, we may not want to count someone as having little freedom to play professional basketball solely because his own estimate is low of his making the cut. Certainly we would not want to say that someone is highly free to play professional basketball just because he thinks that his chances are good.

So, more objective probabilities seem appropriate to most non-coercive situations and "agent probabilities" to coercive situations. One can, of course, make use of objective probabilities in conjunction with a degree of freedom account for coercive situations and agent probabilities in non-coercive situations, but typically one will have to alert one's audience or risk misunderstanding. There is a respect in which the teller was quite free not to hand over the money, but it is not the respect that is usually the focus of attention in such cases.

Concerned as we now are with the freedom to perform a particular action in a particular setting, we can afford to be tolerant of different approaches to probability, picking whichever one seems most appropriate to the agent's and the conversation's context. When it comes to the agent's or society's total freedom, a more uniform treatment of probability will be called for, and that will require another, and slightly more detailed, look at the probability issue, in Section 13.

Even after having given a satisfactory account of the appropriate notion of probability in a given context, the view that freedom varies with probability has some difficulties. For example, we would not usually want to say of an eligible ticket-holder in a fair sweepstakes that he or she has a low degree of freedom to win the prize. There are good reasons we do not talk this way. We all know that the chances of winning a sweepstakes are small. We could put this fact into the language of unfreedom, but we would not gain anything by so doing. So we save that language for asserting such matters as that our ticketholder is ineligible to win, perhaps because of being related to the sweepstakes administrators.

But suppose that an indigent dishwasher has a sweepstakes ticket and plans to retire to the Riviera if he wins, or if any similar windfall comes his way. There may not be much point in saying that he is not very free to win the sweepstakes, but there is some point in saying that he is not very free to retire to the Riviera. The reason that the latter claim has a point is, of course, that some people have much better chances of retiring to the Riviera, if they choose to do so, than does our dishwasher. For some, to borrow a metaphor of Berlin's, the door leading to the Riviera is wide open. For the dishwasher it is open just a crack.

Sometimes low probability freedoms are of significant value to the individual. For example, the freedom to become president of the country may give some people a feeling of greater personal worth. Losing this freedom would not change the course of my life, but it would be a political slap in the face. And our dishwasher's freedom to retire to the Riviera by winning the sweepstakes might represent the one ray of hope in his life.

Still, however much the possession of a low probability freedom may be worth as a psychological matter, it can hardly be counted as a very serious addition to the individual's total stock of freedom, when we turn to that topic in Chapter IV.

CHAPTER III

THE FREEDOM TO DO A PARTICULAR THING: THE SUBJECTIVE SIDE

The distinction between objective and subjective factors involved in the agent's freedom to do something is at best rough. While restraint and incapacity are, for the most part, clearly objective matters, coercion just as clearly brings in elements from the subjective side – the intentions of the coercer and the beliefs of the coercee. This showed up again in the discussion of probability, where either objective or subjective probabilities are relevant, depending on the context.

So I will be shifting the focus of attention only slightly in considering in more detail the relation of the agent's beliefs and information to his or her freedom to do x. The relation of other aspects of the agent's psychology to this freedom will then take us farther into the subjective side of freedom.

8. BELIEF AND INFORMATION

The two fundamental questions about the relation of belief to freedom are these. When, if ever, is A free (to a high degree) to do x if A does not believe it is possible for A to do x? When is A not free to do x if A believes it is possible for A to do x?

The second question is the easier one. As a first approximation, A is not free to do x if A *wrongly* believes that it is possible for A to do x. If I am imprisoned, my false belief that I can escape by picking the lock does not make me free.

Let me add a little more detail to the above formulation. If A believes that it is possible for A to do x, but it is, in fact, not possible because of the existence of w, then if w is a (defining) preventing condition of freedom, A is not free to do x. On the negative account of freedom, then, such a w would be a human interference; restraint, coercion, force or the like. On a positive account, w could range more widely. In fact, nearly anything would count *except* certain of A's psychological states and perhaps certain psychological states of other persons. These exceptions will come in for discussion in Section 9. In any event, there will be cases, on any account, where A wrongly believes it is possible for A to do x, yet

A is free to do *x*. These will be cases where what makes *A*'s belief false is not a preventing condition of freedom. Even in these cases, then, false belief does not *make* one free.

It is more plausible that having no belief that something is possible might eliminate an alternative than that a false belief in possibility might open up an alternative. Consider an extreme case. I am going to contend that there is a kind of possibility under which it would have been possible for the ancient Phoenicians to have built a reasonably powerful optical microscope. Suppose that we have a panel of metallurgical and optical engineers and technicians together with historians of science and technology. I suppose that this panel, given enough time and only those materials and tools available to the ancient Phoenicians (but as much of these as they needed) could succeed in building a crude microscope sufficiently powerful to make out, say, amoebae. Now if the panel of contemporary experts could build a microscope using Phoenician materials, then presumably they could teach the ancient Phoenicians themselves to do so by giving step-by-step instructions. The most difficult part might be the transmission of certain manual skills, but presumably this could be accomplished through a carefully designed set of preparatory exercises. (Remember that I am allowing considerable time for the completion of the project as well as allowing it unlimited amounts of Phoenician resources and labor.)

But if the Phoenicians, following the step-by-step instructions of our experts, could have built a microscope, then it follows that there is a complex sequence of actions that the Phoenicians could have carried out, which would have produced a microscope. Of course, the Phoenicians without the instructions of our panel of experts would have had no reason to perform this sequence of actions, and it is nearly inconceivable that they should. Still, there was no physical barrier to their doing so (except insofar as their system of knowledge and belief is taken to be physical). In this respect, they could have built a microscope and studied amoebae.

But this is obviously an extravagant use of "could." To say that the ancient Phoenicians were *free* (to any significant degree) to make a microscopic study of amoebae would be even more extravagant and, in almost any context, highly misleading. It would be nearly as misleading to say that I am free to write The Great American Novel, just because there is a sequence of typewriter key pressings which I could make and which would eventuate in that result. An alternative which would be open if only one knew about it may, nonetheless, be effectively quite closed indeed.

On the other hand, not every absence of belief on *A*'s part in the possibility of doing *x* is sufficient for *A* to be unfree to do *x*. Suppose that, as the result of a massive delusion, Henry believes that he will be shot down if he tries to enter a grocery store. Tired of living in constant fear, he decides to end it all by resolutely walking toward the entrance of the local supermarket. Henry believes that he is unfree to enter the supermarket, but he is wrong as he will shortly discover when, with clenched teeth, he makes the last few steps through the door.

Beliefs in the impossibility of doing x which prevent A from trying to do x are, of course, a different matter. The question whether such beliefs should be counted as preventing conditions must be handled cautiously. As already suggested, a reasonable belief that A would be prevented from doing x by the carrying out of a threat should usually be taken to be a preventing condition. On the other hand, unreasonable beliefs, even when they prevent A from doing x, do not always make A unfree to do x. If Henry had stayed away from grocery stores as the result of his delusion, we would not, solely by virtue of that fact, agree with him, in every context, that he was unfree to enter grocery stores. To be sure, there might be contexts where we would agree with Henry. There is a perfectly good psychiatric usage in which delusions and compulsions are said to make one unfree. But if in a discussion of the inadequacy of police protection, Henry alleges that he is not even free to go to the grocery store, we will have to disagree. His ill-founded belief is not a preventing condition on the kinds of freedom appropriate to the context.

Let me now turn to a slightly less bizarre case. Suppose Isabel and June are on the eighth floor of a burning building. They are trying to decide on a means of escape. Isabel goes to check the stairs and returns to report that they are blocked by flames. She declares that the only way is to jump to the roof of the neighboring building, a maneuver she then successfully executes. June, having no reason to doubt Isabel's report and threatened by the advancing flames, elects to jump as well. Tragically, she does not make it – a tragedy compounded by the fact that her desperate leap was unnecessary. Isabel had lied about the stairway which, though smoky, was unblocked and via which escape would have been possible. The lie was calculated to secure just the consequence it had in fact – June's fatal jump.

Was June free (to a high degree) to escape by the stairs? There may be some point in saying that she was. That is, one might express the fact that escape was physically possible via the stairs by saying that June was free to use the stairs, though she didn't know it. But this would be slightly strained and a little misleading. June's belief that the stairs were blocked was reasonable on the evidence. To say that she was free to use the stairs suggests that she had a larger share in the responsibility for her fatal leap than she had. Because we want to ascribe a significant share of the responsibility to Isabel – in fact, criminal responsibility – we do not, without considerable qualification, want to describe June's jump as having been exclusively her own choice. Nor, for that same reason, do we want to say, without a good deal of qualification, that she was free (to a high degree) to go down the stairs.

One might conclude at this point that *reasonable* impossibility beliefs that prevent A from trying to do x make A unfree to do x, while unreasonable ones do so only when the context (and use of "free") has a psychological focus. But this generalization is not quite right.

Suppose that I elect not to run in the Boston Marathon because I believe, on good grounds, that I would not last the distance. Suppose further, however, that my belief is incorrect, though reasonable. Clearly I was free (to a high degree) to start the marathon (in the "unofficial section"). Was I also free to run the marathon? I would have run it if I had chosen to try. And even the very reasonable belief that I would not make it is not an overwhelmingly weighty consideration in the decision whether to make the attempt. These factors lead me to conclude that it is less misleading to say that I was free (to a high degree) to run the marathon than it would be to say that I was unfree. It is not clear to me whether my false belief made me somewhat less free to run. I tend to think that it didn't, even though it was the reason I didn't run.

Notice the key differences between this last case and that of June's leap. June's reasonable belief that the stairs were blocked was a very weighty factor, together with the immediacy of the danger, in her decision not to try the stairs. The belief removes much of her responsibility for the decision to jump. However crucial it may have been in my decision not to attempt the marathon, the reasonable belief that I could not make the distance clearly lacks the force of June's belief. It would remove little of my responsibility for my decision even if I had been told by an authority that I would be reduced to walking before the fifteenth mile. (The case would be very different, again, if the authority told me I would have a heart attack.)

I conjecture, then, that even a reasonable impossibility belief that leads to A's decision not to try to do x is a preventing condition of freedom only when that belief is a weighty factor in the decision – perhaps in the sense that given the belief, the other decision would be unreasonable. At the very least, it seems safe to conclude that reasonable impossibility beliefs diminish freedom more than do unreasonable ones. And weighty reasonable beliefs restrict freedom more than do non-weighty reasonable beliefs. I was freer to run the marathon than June was to use the stairs.

The relevance of A's beliefs to A's freedom to do x requires any political philosophy which emphasizes freedom to be concerned about the channels of information in a society. Manipulation of information may not only diminish freedom but also the autonomy of the agent as in June's case. To think that Isabel acquires responsibility for June's decision to jump is to think that Isabel at least partially undermined June's autonomy. The final decision was, of course, June's. But then the final decision would also have been hers if, with no fire, Isabel ordered her to jump while holding a gun to June's head.

Philosophers, as it happens, have not given much attention to the manipulation of information as it affects freedom and autonomy. Probably the following view of E.F. Carritt is close to being the philosophical consensus on this issue.

It seems clear that our freedom is not impaired by the withholding of useful information, and I am inclined to think not even by the giving of false information. That wrongs us in some other way. I should say that drugging a man, or (if that is possible) hypnotizing him against his will impaired his freedom, but I am inclined to think that propaganda, excitement by rhetoric, music and similar tricks do not.[1]

Carritt's view, which he does not further argue, is in sharp contflict with my conclusions above. Let me put those conclusions in a little further perspective by giving the beginnings of a theory of information, freedom, and autonomy.

It is, I think, best to understand the process of information transmission as potentially part of any decision which relies heavily upon that information. Steps of that process become actual parts of the decision, understood as the conscious guiding of action, wherever they purposively and effectively influence the final decision in a particular direction. Decisions about how information is to be gathered (or invented), edited, summarized, or assessed can sometimes so tip the scales that the final decision by the consumer of the information is little more than a formality. In such cases the information handlers have to take some responsibility for that decision and the autonomy of the final decision maker is diminished. This seems particularly plausible where there was conscious manipulative intent on the part of the information handlers. The decision may be effectively stolen by those located further up the informational stream. It is not plausible to say this where their handling of the information was methodologically sound. In such cases, the information transmission process might be thought of as "transparent" and the final decision retains its integrity.

The infringement of autonomy through the misleading handling of evidence need not take the form of lying. Any special editing of the evidence to make an alternative look more or less attractive than it would on a methodologically sound treatment threatens to co-opt the final decision. Even making factual *truths* appear more plausible than they would on a methodologically sound treatment is misleading. Bad procedures sometimes happen to lead toward the truth: they are still bad procedures.

The misleading need not be intended to mislead. It need not even be intended to control or influence decisions. Handling information under the guidance of a controversial theory, or a theory which would be controversial, if people were not discouraged from challenging it, may have the same effects as intentional misleading. In such cases, the departure from methodological soundness lies in not handling the information in a way neutral among the theories within the realm of controversy. Or, since that is often impossible or too demanding, the methodological unsoundness may be charged to the absence of alternatives sources of information. The individual purveyor of information may not be culpable in such a case. It is the overall system of information transmission that leads to the diminution of autonomy.

If this is correct, then the management of information through control of the educational system and media by persons of a single political outlook may diminish the autonomy of those who base decisions upon that information. If the management of information leads people to fail to perceive alternatives to action or think them significantly less desirable than they otherwise would, then there will be a loss of liberty as well. This seems obviously to be the case in states with strong one party dictatorships. It might also occur where common social backgrounds lead to substantial political agreement on the part of private individuals who control the dispersal of information to a society.

For example, there is a shared belief by owners of newspapers and broadcast networks and stations in the United States that, in general, only members of the Republican and Democratic parties are serious and responsible candidates for public office. This affects the way political news is handled by these media. The handling of news in turn affects the extent to which people hear about the platforms and programs of "fringe" candidates.[2] Those people who would give serious consideration to the views of the fringe candidates, if they knew them, have lost some liberty. Even those who would not seriously consider the views of the fringe candidates may have lost autonomy in not having the information on which properly to make their decision. So a "free press" in all the senses relevant to the autonomy and liberty of its readers must be more than a press which is not controlled by the government. The political correctness of those who control the news is no defense against the charge of unfreedom. Nor it is a defense that everything reported is true. (Some policy recommendations based on this conclusion will appear in Section 17.)

9. PSYCHOLOGICAL BARRIERS, AUTONOMY, AND FREEDOM

I understand an autonomous decision to be a decision which is genuinely the agent's own decision. It is not made or forced upon the agent by anyone else. It stands as an act of individual moral sovereignty.

As a principle of first approximation, behavior must be at least partially autonomous for society to hold the individual responsible for it and its consequences. To take Aristotle's example, I am not responsible for damage I may cause when I am blown around by an irresistible wind. This is only a principle of first approximation, however, because, as Aristotle noted, I may acquire responsibility by virtue of autonomous choices which placed me in such a position that my non-autonomous behavior would forseeably have certain consequences. For example, if I carry a fragile statue along a path which I know to be subject to extreme winds, I may not disclaim responsibility for the loss when the wind knocks me against a boulder, breaking the statue. Responsibility for putting any agent, including oneself, in a non-autonomous situation will, under certain circumstances, extend to a responsibility for the consequences of the non-autonomous situation. (The same will turn out to be true of cases where the agent is autonomous but of diminished competence.)

In addition to its close tie with responsibility, autonomy is a necessary condition of freedom. If I am not in a position autonomously to choose to do x, then I am not in a position to *do* x at all. Putting things this way does require us to distinguish, again, between things which happen to me and things which I do. Caught in Aristotle's wind storm, I am not free to enter my front door, and this remains the case even if the wind blows me through that door. So 'A exhibits behavior x at time t' does not contradict 'A is not free to do x at time t.' However, 'A does x at time t' does contradict 'A is not free to do x at time t.'

The simplest condition of non-autonomy is unconsciousness. At least let us assume that when one is unconscious, one makes no choices. (This may require that dreaming not be counted as a state of unconsciousness for these purposes.) If I am unconscious, there may still be things I am free to do. For example, go sailing the next day. But there is nothing I am free to do *at that time*. (Again, "lie there in a heap" will not count as something I *do*.)

Given that unconsciousness is a sufficient condition for non-autonomy and that diminished or impaired consciousness (insanity and the like) is usually regarded as among the standard cases of non-autonomy as well, it might be conjectured that "high grade consciousness" is a sufficient condition of autonomy. But that conjectural leap would, apparently, fall short. To take a religious fiction case, suppose that A is possessed by a demon which makes all the decisions about A's behavior while A continues to experience normally as a passive observer. It is easy enough to imagine all A's bodily behavior being controlled by the demon, but that is not quite enough. The demon must also take charge of A's mental life, at least so far as preventing A from exercising any control over it. In fact, the demon must even prevent A from making ineffective choices about either bodily behavior or mental behavior. You may think offhand that it is a little hard to picture what it would be like to have a mental life at a normal level of intelligence, understanding, and the like, but no choice at all. Probably, however, you have experienced a situation something like this, at least briefly, while absorbed in a book or movie. It is not necessary that we imagine the consciousness being "merely receptive" in the sense of having only contents which come from "the outside" via sensation. Memory and imagination can take place as well: it will just not be the case that the agent *chooses* to remember or imagine this or that. Though out of the ordinary, there seems nothing incoherent about a high state of consciousness which is nonetheless entirely non-autonomous.

A more ordinary, but partial, case of rational non-autonomy is that of coercion. As already discussed, if A hands over ten dollars as the result of being threatened at gun point by B, we do not want to say that A was free to keep the money. Nor would we usually want to say that A's decision to give the money to B is autonomous. The situation is, however, complicated. We might well want to say that A's decision to give the money to B *rather than risk being shot* was autonomous. No one interfered with A's making up his or her own mind on whether or not to risk being shot. But, paradoxically, the decision not to risk getting shot was, in one perfectly good sense, the same decision as the decision to hand over the money. How can the same decision be both autonomous and non-autonomous?

There are at least two different ways to handle this difficulty. One is to say that the notion of autonomy applies to decisions under particular descriptions. The same decision can be autonomous under one description and non-autonomous under another, just as the same person might be believed by A to take part in cabinet meetings under the description "The Vice President" but not under the description "The Presiding Officer of the Senate." In Quine's terminology,[3] this would be to say that autonomy contexts, like belief contexts, are opaque rather than transparent. On this treatment, a decision will be non-autonomous by virtue of coercion under a given description if that description does not mention the threatened alternative. If the description does mention the threatened alternative, then the coercive threat does not make the decision non-autonomous under that description.

The other reasonably attractive way out of the paradox is to say that the decision to turn over the ten dollars is autonomous. After all, it is an action which A does intentionally and with full knowledge. Moreover, it is an action A could be praised or blamed for. (In this case we would most likely praise A for behaving rationally and prudently.) It might sound odd to say that A was *responsible* for turning over the ten dollars, because that language would normally be used to say that A was to be blamed for the loss of the money. But the fact that we would not blame A in this case is not because the decision was beyond praise and blame, but because it was neutral or praiseworthy.

It probably would not make too much difference which of these two courses we take so long as we do it explicitly and consistently. We just end up with slightly different ways of using "autonomy." The transparent reading is slightly cleaner, but I will adopt the opaque reading. It is, I think, less natural to say that a decision which is forced upon me coercively is still just as much *my* decision as is a non-forced decision. So I will say that A's decision to turn over the ten dollars was not autonomous although his choice to turn over the ten dollars rather than risk being shot was autonomous. I hope this now sounds no more paradoxical than that A turned over the ten dollars unwillingly, though A was more than willing to turn over the ten dollars rather than be shot.

Full deliberative rationality is not, then, a sufficient condition of autonomy. But is it a necessary condition? Philosophers of idealist persuasion have been convinced that it is. Members of the negative tradition have typically thought that it is not. This is not to say that negative libertarians believe that non-standard mental states are never barriers to autonomy and freedom. Hypnotism and insanity, for example, are taken by nearly everyone to limit autonomy and freedom. But the negative tradition seems to hold that one can sometimes be autonomous and free even though one is not fully rational. It seems to me that the negative tradition is right about this. In fact, I think that tradition may not have gone quite far enough in ascribing autonomy and freedom to those in non-normal states of consciousness.

Let me start with hypnotism, a case in which the popular ascription of non-autonomy and unfreedom may well be wrong. It seems initially that a successful post-hypnotic suggestion not to do x, where x is something A otherwise would have done, makes A unfree to do x and non-autonomous in doing not-x. Since, however, hypnotic suggestions are not always effective, they presumably are sometimes resistible. If A on one occasion resists a suggestion which A follows on another occasion, we reasonably suspect that A may have been free to do something other than it on the first occasion as well. Perhaps the questions of freedom and autonomy in the face of hypnosis ought to turn on the strength of the suggestion vis à vis the subject's own inclination. If A was predisposed to do y, indifferent towards y, or mildly disinclined to do y, then we have little or no reason to believe that the "successful" hypnotic suggestion to do y compromised A's autonomy. If, however, the suggestion overcomes a strong determination on A's part not to do y, then it seems that A is not free not to do y or autonomous in doing y. If it is true, as some experts have claimed, that hypnotism never overcomes strong determinations, then hypnotism is less a barrier to freedom and autonomy than philosophers have sometimes conceded.

Insanity's relation to freedom and autonomy is even more difficult to discuss than that of hypnotism because insanity is such a disparate group of phenomena, unified more at the level of symptoms than at the level of underlying causes – and unified very little at the level of symptoms.

One possibility that suggests itself is that whenever we explain A's doing x in terms of A's mental illness, then A's autonomy in doing x and freedom not to do x were at least diminished. Of course, it has to be the right sort of explanation. A's going to see a psychiatrist would presumably be explained in terms of A's mental illness, but might itself be an entirely rational action. However, even when we have the right sort of explanations so that we have segregated the "crazy" actions, the character of the particular explanations involved might lead to the conclusion that the agent is autonomous after all. I suppose people behave in deviant ways from any number of different causes including, though not limited to, strong non-normal desires and aversions, crazy beliefs, and inability to carry elementary reasoning through successfully. Let me divide these into two categories – non-normal desires and incompetence.

Strong non-normal desires and aversions may make someone a misfit in society without affecting that person's autonomy. If A is otherwise normal but for a consuming desire to somersault down the street naked, it seems to me probable that A somersaults autonomously and is free to act otherwise. I am not much moved by the consideration that, given the strength of A's desire, A could not have done otherwise. Given my desire to give my lecture this morning, it might be said that I could not have done otherwise either. Suppose that the only relevant difference (besides its social acceptability) between A's desire to somersault and mine to lecture is the intensity of the desire. As a general proposition, it seems that if B would rather do x than y, then an unmanipulated, absolute,[4] increase in the attractiveness of x to B ought never, by itself, make B unfree to do y or non-autonomous in doing x. Strong desires make for easy choices, but easy choices are just as good choices as hard choices.

Our somersaulter is very likely to be institutionalized, and it may be reassuring to think that we have not thereby sacrificed the freedom of an autonomous agent. It is reassuring to believe that anyone who is properly placed in a mental institution was non-autonomous or, at best, of limited autonomy. But I suspect that this belief is incorrect.

Of course, it may be that people with powerful desires often wish that they could resist those desires. Such people are, then, divided against themselves on the choice of *x*, and this does offer a *possible* grounds for ascribing to them a defect in autonomy. One might say that such a decision by its nature represents *A* only partially. *A* cannot identify with it unequivocally. It would not be plausible to ascribe a defect in autonomy in every case where the individual's desires come into conflict. We certainly do not want to end up saying that easy decisions are always more autonomous than hard ones. We often take special pride in our "ownership" of hard decisions.

But hard decisions come in at least two kinds. In one case, after sorting out and evaluating the considerations on all sides, I come to a decision which, however close it may be, is my undivided conclusion. In other cases I regret, or inwardly condemn a decision, even as I am making it. Or I wish that I were making another decision. This does not always happen in cases of conflicting desires, but it may happen. It is evidence of the fact that normal human consciousness is not entirely unitary.

It has sometimes been assumed that the paradigmatic case of being of two minds about a decision is that of giving in to short term pleasure as against the carrying out of long run plans. And while this is a frequent occurrence for most of us, the opposite takes place as well. We wish, while bending to the call of duty, that we had instead decided to go skiing. In this case, it will typically not be my "rational," "higher," self condemning a decision resulting from my "lower" nature, but just the opposite. If being of two minds in the first case is to count as a defect in autonomy, it ought also in the other.

So if there is sometimes a reason of the divided mind sort for ascribing less than full autonomy and freedom to those driven by strong desires, this need not always be the case for those with strong non-normal desires. If they do not struggle against and condemn those desires, but follow them single-mindedly, I fail to see any reason to regard them as less autonomous than those of us who have more normal desires. Moreover, if being of "two minds" does count as a defect in autonomy, it ought to count as just as much a defect when the more rational self wins the dispute or when the sides cannot be sorted out in terms of rationality.

Present considerations do not, then, give any general reasons for doubting the autonomy and freedom of those who count as insane by virtue of strong abnormal desires. Nor do they support the more general view that autonomy requires rationality.

Crazy behavior that has its cause in eccentric beliefs or inability to reason presents the possibility of a variant of the "divided mind" defect in autonomy. If *A* has false beliefs, *A* may choose to do *x* to achieve result *y*. But doing *x* may not achieve *y*. It might even be that doing *x* precludes y, while not doing x would lead to y. In such a case, one might be tempted to say that A's doing x, being contrary to A's own real intentions, does not accurately represent A. There will be a sense in which it was not A's decision; namely, a sense in which we describe the decision in terms of its consequences and then construe the context opaquely. A did not choose to do something that would result in not-y, though what he choose did have that result.

In cases of this sort, if the failure to perceive consequences properly is due to crazy beliefs or dramatic inability to reason properly, that may, in circumstances seriously dangerous to A, provide justification for "paternalistically" intervening to prevent A's doing x. (This will be discussed further in Section 32.) We may also want to say, depending on the circumstances, that A was not morally responsible for the consequences of A's actions. Moral responsibility requires some ability to understand consequences. All this has sometimes been taken to show that decisions running contrary to the agent's real purposes, based on crazy beliefs or dramatically faulty reasoning, are not autonomous decisions. I am inclined to doubt this conclusion so long as autonomy is identified with the agent's "ownership" of the decision. (Of course, if "autonomy" is understood in terms of moral responsibility, then the conclusion is trivial.) The reason I am inclined to doubt it is that the only defect I see in the agent's ownership of the decision is that he or she decided (opaquely) to do something which would result in rather than exclude y. But this situation is one we all find ourselves in frequently. Our intentions often miscarry. This may happen as the result of crazy beliefs or incompetence, but it usually has more mundane causes. So if we were to say that this sort of defect means dimimished autonomy, we should have to say the same thing about all kinds of "normal" decisions as well as crazy ones. Only omniscience would insure autonomy. We may, then, safely reject this requirement of appropriateness to real ends as too strong.

For similar reasons, a false assessment of x's consequences does not, by itself, make one unfree to do x, even if it results from crazy beliefs or highly incompetent reasoning. These sorts of mental defects may undermine moral responsibility, and they may make institutionalization permissible, but they do not entail that the agent is non-autonomous or unfree to act other than he or she did act. Of course, if some other person manipulates a mind given to crazy beliefs or incompetent reasoning, that might undermine autonomy and freedom. But manipulation can undermine the autonomy of normal people as well, as I argued last section.

So far I have not found any convincing reasons for considering the autonomy of the insane to be less than that of other people. Nor have I found reasons for taking them to have less than normal freedom to do what they did not in fact do (assuming they were not externally prevented from so doing). I would not, however, want to say that the unmanipulated insane are *never* less autonomous because of their mental states. It may well be that some mental disorders are of such nature that it is implausible to think of the behavior as coming from anything which could reasonably be called a choice or decision. In such cases, there would be neither autonomy nor freedom. My suspicion is that mental patients are probably thought of in this way much too often. Again, it makes us feel better about the way they are treated. But since there may well be some cases that really do fit this picture, I do not claim that the unmanipulated insane are always autonomous.

My chief purpose in giving so much attention to insanity is to counter the idealist doctrine that only decisions made with deliberative rationality are autonomous. Of course, some philosophers simply identify autonomy with rationality. I doubt, however, that autonomy as rationality has much independent interest. We have a perfectly good word for rationality. And autonomy as rationality seems to be neither necessary nor sufficient for moral responsibility. We certainly often want to hold people responsible for actions resulting when their desires win out over their rational preferences. But my main objection to autonomy as rationality is simply that it corresponds poorly with what I, again, take to be the root notion of autonomy – that the decision really is the agent's own decision. The view that my rationality is "really me" while my desires are not is, I think, pure prejudice. I may, when rational, prefer my rational "higher self" to my "lower self" thought of as those desires which sometimes tempt me from my rationally thought out plans. But I do not see any reason to take the lower self to be any less me than the higher self. If anything, my "merely empirical desires" seem a more constant feature of my character over time than either my powers of rational deliberation or the interests, purposes, and plans which emerge from such deliberation.

The best argument for identifying the higher self with the autonomous self seemed to me to be an argument from insanity. If we were to accept the common view that the behavior of the severely mentally ill is non-autonomous, it would be tempting to conclude that extreme irrationality is incompatible with autonomy. It is implausible that there should be a cut off point on the scale of rationality. So it would seem that the degree of autonomy ought to decrease as rationality decreases. Thus only our rational decisions would be fully autonomous.

I have tried to cut this argument off at its source by arguing that not even extreme irrationality entails the absence of autonomy. Non-decision entails the absence of autonomy, but not irrational decision. The best way to turn aside my counterargument might be to show the less rational a decision is, the less it counts as a decision at all. I see ways such an argument might get started, but I do not think it could be carried through successfully.

If my position turns out to be correct, then people suffering under such temporary incompetencies as drunkenness will also be autonomous. Recall, again, however, that this does not entail that they will be morally responsible for all their actions. Typically, I think, they will be, but if A were made drunk by B genuinely against A's will (say at gunpoint), then B would be held responsible for actions resulting from A's incompetence – even if they were autonomous actions of A.

There are psychological states that undermine autonomy and freedom. They include states in which no decision can be ascribed to the agent, not even an ill-considered or unconsidered decision. They also include cases where other persons successfully manipulate an agent in a state of diminished competence. But they do not, if I am right, include all cases in which the agent is not morally responsible for his or her actions. And "higher selves" and deliberative rationality do not get a better score with respect to autonomy or freedom than do "lower selves" and spontaneous or "irrational" actions.

10. THE DESIRE TO DO x

It is a theme that runs through most of the negative tradition that one is not made unfree by constraints against an undesired action. Recall that Hobbes defined freedom only for those things which the agent "has a will to do." Locke's famous formulation ran: "that ill deserves the name of confinement which hedges us in only from bogs and precipices."[5] In discussing the permissibility of forcibly preventing someone from crossing an unsafe bridge, where there is not time for a warning, Mill asserted, "liberty consists in doing what one desires, and he does not desire to fall into the river."[6] Russell echoed the same point: "Freedom in general may be defined as the absence of obstacles to the realization of desires."[7]

Some members of the negative tradition, however, have rejected the majority view of the connection between liberty and wanting to do the action in question. In the original version of "Two Concepts of Liberty," for example, Berlin wrote, "If I am prevented by other persons from doing what I want I am to that degree unfree . . ."[8] In the revised version this became: If I am prevented by others from doing what I could otherwise do, I am to that degree unfree . . ."[9]

Berlin's change of mind on this issue seems to me sound. There are serious problems in trying to make any simple connection between desire and either A's being a free person or A's being free to do x. I will continue with the theme of this chapter by considering first, and in most detail, this second, and simpler, sort of ascription of freedom. One possibility is this:

(1) A is free to do x if and only if A desires to do x and there are no constraints (of the appropriate sorts) which prevent A from doing x.

But, understanding "not free" to entail "unfree," (1) would require us to say that you are unfree to stand up when the only reason that you don't stand up is that you don't want to. This was certainly not the link between desire and freedom that Locke or Mill had in mind. Perhaps more in line with tradition:

(2) A is free to do x if and only if, if A desires to do x, then there are no constraints (of the appropriate sorts) which prevent A from doing x.

The problem with this formulation, understood in the light of standard propositional logic, is that it makes one free to do anything which one has no desire to do. But I am not free to burn the Mona Lisa, nor is the contented prisoner free to leave prison. Perhaps the best that can be done along these lines is as follows:

(3) A is free to do x if and only if A desires to do x and there are no constraints (of the appropriate sorts) which prevent A from doing x. A is unfree to do x if and only if A desires to do x and there are constraints (of the appropriate sorts) which prevent A from doing x.

If A does not desire to do x, then A is neither free nor unfree to do x. The question of freedom does not arise. On this formulation, we do not get the absurdities that I was unfree to stand up a minute ago or that the contented prisoner is free to leave prison. But what we do get is that I was neither free nor unfree to stand up and that the prisoner is neither free nor unfree to leave. And surely these consequences are very little to be preferred.

   If we represent the possibilities on a chart, the predicament of the simple link between desire and being free to do a particular thing becomes clear.

	desires to do x	does not desire to do x
constrained from doing x	unfree	?
unconstrained from doing x	free	?

The two western corners of this matrix are filled in following the basic idea of negative libertarianism. Similarly, we can rule out putting "free" in the northeast together with "unfree" in the southeast, since constraint is obviously not emancipatory for the negative tradition. Filling both the open positions with "unfree" gives (1), and the problem of the "unfree to stand" case. Filling the open positions with "free" gives (2), which has the odd consequence that if you are not free to do x, then you want to do x. It runs afoul of the contented prisoner. Putting "neither free nor unfree" into both blanks is (3), which gets into trouble both in denying that I was free to stand up a minute ago and in denying that the contented prisoner is unfree to depart.

The final and best possibility is to assign "unfree" to the northeast and "free" to the southeast. But then desire drops out altogether as a defining condition of freedom and unfreedom. In fact this is, I think, exactly what the negative tradition should do in characterizing an individual's freedom to perform a particular action. We get a simpler and overall more plausible account, given the root ideas of negative liberty, if the presence or absence of constraint does all the work.

While I think the negative account could do perfectly well without mentioning desire in the case of freedom to perform particular actions, desire may not be quite so easily dispensed with from an account of the total freedom of a person. So let me anticipate this topic a little and run quickly through some possible simple ways of linking desire and the individual's total freedom.

(4) A is free if and only if there is at least one action x which A desires to do and there are no constraints (of the appropriate sorts) which prevent A from doing x.

This would require us to say that a temporarily apathetic person faced with a wide variety of quite unconstrained options is unfree or at least non-free. This is implausible and, I think, quite unacceptable to the negative tradition. (4) also has the problem of ascribing freedom to the contented prisoner.

(5) A is free if and only if there are no constraints (of the appropriate sorts) on any action which A desires to perform.

This eliminates the ascription of total unfreedom to the apathetic individual or the stoic saint, but at the cost of ascribing unfreedom to anyone who has *any* desire that is blocked in one of the appropriate ways. But if Walter Mitty has a secret fantasy desire to rob a bank, the constraints against bank robbing do not make Walter an unfree person: they only make him unfree to rob the bank.

For the most part, these problems, affecting any simple link between desire and freedom, have gone unnoticed or ignored. Desire is brought in to solve some specific problem, such as Mill's hazardous bridge. Then it is dismissed from mind. One member of the tradition who faced squarely up to the desire problems was E.F. Carritt. Carritt gave a characterization of liberty as "the power of doing what one would choose without interference by other persons."[10] Now this need not be a negative account at all, nor one tied to desire in an objectionable way. But the way Carritt took "power" and "interference," it turns out negative, and the way he took "would choose" establishes the simple link to desire. Carritt dealt with the desire problem as follows:

A penal law against murder, then, limits freedom of all who want to murder but not of others.[11]

And:

If by long custom people actually prefer and petition to remain slaves, or if they cease even to wish to enjoy what is in the occupation of others, then their slavery or exclusion does not diminish their freedom, unless they change their mind. We may call them free fools and blame somebody for their folly.[12]

Though it is surely sensible to say that homicide statutes restrict all of us (after all, they apply to everyone within the jurisdiction), it is also sensible to say, with Carritt, that such laws restrict only potential murderers. (But I wonder whether they restrict all potential murderers, only the ones who take the law into their calculations, or only the ones who, because they take the law into their calculations, do not become actual murderers.)

What is less easy to accept is that contented slaves or inmates are free. This flies in the face of at least most ordinary language. Of more concern, it seems completely incompatible with the whole thrust of the negative tradition. Most seriously of all, it hopelessly weakens the moral indictment we can bring against slavery where the slaves are so thoroughly propagandized as to accept their condition willingly. We want to be able to say that there is something seriously and unacceptably wrong with slavery even if the slaves are not foolish in accepting it so far as a rational evaluation of their desires and prospects is concerned. Slavery is wrong because it destroys freedom and autonomy, however conducive it may be to the welfare of the slaves.

To sum up, the desire condition causes all sorts of trouble for the negative account of liberty. As already suggested, negative libertarians would be well advised simply to drop it in the case of freedom to perform a particular action. The complete dispensability of the desire condition is somewhat more problematic in a negative account of "free person" or "free society," however.

We do not want to count someone as free if there are a number of alternatives (lacking constraints of the appropriate sorts) but all of which are very unappealing. For example, one imprisoned in a tower may become resigned or try to overpower the heavily armed jailors or try to jump to safety from the 200' high window or turn in all his or her friends to be tortured in exchange for release. Such a person, despite the many things he or she is free to do, is not free.

Proponents of the negative account have seen that one needs to bring in states like desire or choice to give a correct account of freedom in such cases. The mistake was to bring in desire in too simple a way. The better course is to take desirability and related matters as affecting the contribution an alternative makes to liberty. But this is to start thinking of liberty in a different way. The emphasis shifts from the constraints to the alternatives and such matters as their range as well as their desirability. The absence of interference by other persons appears as but one feature of liberty among several. Once this corner is turned, the official negative list of preventing conditions begins to look arbitrary. More appealing becomes a positive account of liberty along the lines I will now sketch.

CHAPTER IV

PERSONAL FREEDOM

Having now at hand at least a rough account of what it is for A to be free to degree d to do x, it is time to examine what it is for A to be free to degree d. For certain sorts of moral evaluations all we need to know is the individual's freedom or unfreedom to perform or omit a particular action, but in evaluating the overall desirability of a person's life or of a society's institutions and practices, we would like to know about total freedom. The various things an individual is free to do are obviously components of some sort of his or her total freedom. If there is nothing one is free to do, then clearly one is not free. The present task could be seen as filling in the rest of the part-whole logic of particular freedom and total freedom.

A chief desideratum in putting this account together is to come up with a notion of total freedom which reflects what is valuable about freedom for the individual. Where a choice presents itself, I have construed freedom in such a way that more freedom will tend to be more desirable than less freedom. This strategy cannot, of course, be followed blindly. It is a truism that one cannot pack everything good into the notion of freedom or it becomes hopelessly bloated. Conversely, one cannot give an account of freedom under which it is so "purified" and limited that its increase is always desirable all things considered. To eliminate the possibility of conflict with other values, such a notion of freedom would have to be very lean. In fact, it is doubtful that anything could count as freedom under this strict requirement. So in characterizing freedom roughly as "freedom as valuable for the individual" one is limited both by pre-theoretic intuitions about where, roughly, the boundaries of the domain of freedom lie, and by considerations of the utility of the developed account. But within these constraints there is a good deal of latitude, which I make use of to make the individual's degree of freedom correspond, as much as possible, to what is valuable about freedom for the individual. Much of the difference between positive and negative accounts of freedom arises because the positive account follows this strategy at points where the negative account is guided by other considerations. I will indicate below a few of the instances where these differences surface. The overall relation of positive freedom to value will be addressed in more detail in Chapter VII.

I will approach total individual freedom in two stages. In this chapter I will consider freedom solely from the perspective of the individual. What I will call "personal freedom" is not "political freedom" or "social freedom." It is not in all its details of *direct* interest to the political or social theorist. It *is* of interest to the individual who has it and so, of course, to value theory. Personal freedom is something Robinson Crusoe could have more or less of without the intervention of another human being.

Members of the negative tradition have frequently denied interest in such a notion of freedom because it is not of optimal utility in political philosophy. If you share this view, let me request a little patience. I will use "personal freedom" as a step to "social liberty." The basis structure of the two will be the same except that those features of "personal freedom" which have no relevance to questions of public policy will be edited out of "social liberty." The negative libertarian may still find much to object to in my account of social liberty, but lack of relevance to political theory should not be among the complaints.

11. BERLIN'S FIVE FACTORS

The general structure of total freedom as I understand it is very similar to that which Berlin outlined (for negative freedom!) in "Two Concepts." Since it will be useful to have Berlin's account available for comparison, I will examine it in some detail.

The extent of my freedom seems to depend on (*a*) how many possibilities are open to me (although the method of counting these can never be more than impressionistic. Possibilities of action are not discrete entities like apples, which can be exhaustively enumerated); (*b*) how easy or difficult each of these possibilities is to actualize; (*c*) how important in my plan of life, given my chararacter and circumstances, these possibilities are when compared with each other; (*d*) how far they are closed and opened by deliberate human acts; (*e*) what value not merely the agent, but the general sentiment of the society in which he lives, puts on the various possibilities. All these magnitudes must be "integrated", and a conclusion, necessarily never precise, or indisputable, drawn from this process.[1]

There is a great deal that seems plausible to me about this explication of the extent of the individual's total freedom. In particular, that one is freer the more alternatives one has seems right, at least as a first approximation. Moreover it is reasonable that each alternative's contribution to freedom should depend on such matters as its difficulty and its importance to the individual's life plan.

I have, however, grave doubts about one item in Berlin's account – factor (*d*). The purpose of (*d*) is, of course, to keep the account within the negative tradition. It is the only point on which the positive libertarian must disagree with Berlin. The questions I have about (d) are whether it is compatible with the intuitions underlying the other factors and, in fact, just how it is to be understood in the context of these other factors.

The essential negative claim is usually best understood, as I have urged following MacCallum, as a constraint on preventing conditions; that is, a constraint on what is to count as "closing" a possibility. If A cannot do x for reasons having nothing to do with human interferences, then the negative tradition does not count A as unfree to do x. (Whether A is said to be free to do x or neither free nor unfree to do x will, for certain x's, vary among negative accounts.) So we might see the point of (d) solely as modifying (a). The effect would be the same as if (a) appeared:

(a') how many possibilities are open to me, where a possibility is open unless I am prevented from doing it by deliberate human actions.

This sounds classically negative, but it will not produce the standard negative results when combined with other factors of Berlin's account. Consider my alternative of running a four minute mile. Since I am not prevented from doing this by other persons, it will count as one of my possibilities under (a'). So far, so good. The positive libertarian may balk at saying that I am free to run a four minute mile, but the negative libertarian need not. However, consider now Berlin's factor (b). How difficult would it be for me to run a four minute mile? I blush to admit that when I am in peak condition, and push myself to the limit with an extreme act of will, I am, under the most favorable conditions, lucky to break six minutes. There can, then, be no doubt that it is quite impossible that I should run a four minute mile. So if we represent degree of difficulty on a scale of 0 to 1, with 0 standing for impossibility, I will have a 0 for factor (b) for running four minute miles. The most natural conclusion would be that this possibility does not contribute to my freedom on the present interpretation of Berlin's account. If difficulty decreases an alternative's contribution to liberty, impossibility ought to wipe it out altogether. But of course the conclusion we have ended up with is positive rather than negative in character (as I define those terms). As such, it is not only incompatible with Berlin's stated position, but also incompatible with the presumed intent of (d). Taking (d) to apply only to (a), it is possible to evade its intent by making use of (b).

Perhaps (d) is supposed to apply to (b) as well as (a), filtering out "positive" difficulties. That is, (b) would embrace only those difficulties which are the result of deliberate human actions. So understood, my physical difficulties in running a four minute mile drop out of consideration, and we end up with the negative conclusion that I am free to run a four minute mile. This conclusion is not only one Berlin should feel comfortable with, but one that fits fairly well with the language of (d). The quantitative sounding "how far they are closed or opened" might be a slightly loose way of suggesting an editing process under which such "positive" difficulties as incapacities are dropped from consideration while "negative" ones are retained. Taking (d) to be a constraint on (a) alone, the phrase "how far they are closed" would not seem very appropriate.

If, however, this way of understanding (d) seems to make sense in terms of (a) and (b), there are further problems when we get to (c) and (e). They arise because it is possible to repeat the same tactic which led to the conclusion that (d) must apply to (b) as well as (a). Consider (c). One thing that determines how important an alternative is to my life plan is the balance of costs and benefits associated with that alternative. Suppose alternatives x and y have equal (and significant) benefits and equal (and relatively low) costs resulting from deliberate human actions. So far there is no reason to believe that either x or y would have a privileged place in my life plan. However, x has very great costs which are not the result of deliberate human actions. It leads to an incapacitating disease. y has no such costs. I might for this reason include y, but not x, in my life plan. The positive libertarian will welcome the conclusion that x contributes much less to my freedom than does y. But the negative libertarian ought to feel that positive preventing conditions are being brought in by the back door. In fact, it seems as if the costs attendant on the extreme natural difficulty of an alternative ought to affect both categories (c) and (e) dramatically. So what we tried to rule out by taking (d) to apply to (b) as well as (a) may come right back to haunt us via (c) and (e).

But a way out of this problem presents itself immediately. Surely what we ought to do is to interpret (d) as applying to (c) and (e) as well as to (a) and (b). Applied to (c) and (e), (d) would operate as a constraint on what costs are considered. It is also, perhaps, initially more plausible that (d) should be relevant to all the other factors, rather than just to some of them. After all, it would otherwise have been easier, and clearer, to build the negative constraint directly into the formulation of the particular factors it was understood to modify. Its separate billing can be seen as an indication that it applies wherever the distinction between deliberately caused conditions and other conditions can be applied in our assessment of the extent of freedom.

The problem is that editing out of (c) and (e) all costs which are not due to deliberate human actions changes the character of these categories completely. We get:

(c′) how important in my plan of life these possibilities would be when compared to each other, given my character and circumstances, but abstracting from any differences not due to deliberate human actions.

It is not very easy to know how to perform the abstraction required by (c′). Even if it could be done coherently, it seems highly unlikely that the resulting ranking of actions would have any significance or use. I suppose, abstracting from "merely physical" matters, that trying to walk on water might play as important a role in my life plan as trying to walk on sidewalks. But it is crazy to put the two on a par under a category supposed to be relevant to my life. We just cannot abstract away from all those properties of things which they have naturally (rather than as the result of deliberate human action) and end up with a sensible notion of value or importance to a life plan. Moreover, understanding the role of (d) in this way would destroy the motivation of an "alternatives account" of the sort Berlin gives. The intuition is surely that very difficult alternatives, or alternatives I would never choose under any circumstances, make a smaller addition to the extent of my liberty than do less difficult and more desirable alternatives. This intuition, which seems to me correct, is not sensitive to the source of the difficulty or undesirability. It is this fact which makes (a), (b), (c), and (e), taken together, hard to reconcile with (d).

The only hope for making sense of (d) seems to me to be to think of it, not as eliminating "positive" conditions from the other factors, but as giving special "weight" to deliberate human actions. For example, if x is foreclosed by non-human conditions and y by deliberate human actions, we might say that x makes a small contribution to freedom while y makes none. Or if the difficulties associated with w are non-human and those associated with z the result of deliberate human actions, we might say that w makes a smaller contribution to freedom than does z. This seems a fairly plausible way of understanding Berlin's formulation here. But it does commit Berlin to a thorough-going compromise with the positive account of liberty. One's freedom may be diminished by contingencies having nothing to do with the deliberate actions of other persons. That this concession to positive liberty should appear in the account of the extent of freedom by one of the negative tradition's most eloquent spokesmen, ought to encourage anyone who believes the negative account too narrow. In fact, once this concession is made, there is reason to doubt whether anything is to be gained by giving more weight to negative preventing conditions; except as this makes the account more useful to political theory (a benefit I will secure in a simpler way in the next chapter).

If we understand (d) to operate on the other factors, either (in some way I do not understand) to eliminate positive conditions or (more plausibly) to give them less weight, we could, very roughly, represent the extent of a person's liberty for Berlin as:

$$\sum_{i=0}^{n} b_i \cdot c_i \cdot \dot{e}_i$$

where i enumerates the n possibilities of action (Berlin's (a)); b_i is the difficulty of the ith alternative (represented by a real number between 0 and 1 inclusive, with 0 representing impossibility); c_i is the importance to the individual's life plan (represented by a non-negative real increasing with the importance); and e_i is the value of the ith alternative (represented by a non-negative real increasing with the value). No doubt this oversimplifies Berlin's intentions, but it is a useful model of the general idea behind Berlin's account. What I want to do in the next sections is to develop a similar account (without (d)) which might be represented as follows, as a first approximation:

$$\sum_{i=0}^{n} f_i \cdot v_i \cdot d_i$$

where i, again, enumerates all the individual's alternatives, f_i represents the individual's degree of freedom to perform the ith action (as discussed in Chapters II and III); v_i is the value of the ith alternative, and d_i is a factor representing the degree to which the ith alternative differs from the other alternatives the individual has. (If alternatives could be represented as points in a space with a metric, we might take d_i to be the distance of the ith point from the center of population of the n points.) The above formula would, very neatly, incapsulate the point of the present chapter as arriving at "total personal freedom" by filling in three new factors – the number, variety, and value of the alternatives – which are to be taken together with the previously discussed degree of freedom to do a particular thing. Unfortunately, the situation is not quite that simple. The degree of freedom to do a particular thing already contains value considerations. (Recall, for example, that a threat may count as limiting my freedom to do something unimportant more than it would count as limiting my freedom to do something important.) To avoid counting the same thing in two different places, I will divide up the factors that go into the degree of freedom to do a particular thing. The probability of doing the action will become an independent factor. The lower its probability, the less that alternative contributes (under this heading[2]) to the individual's total freedom. Everything else that affects the degree of freedom to do a particular thing will be consigned to the "value" category, which will also embrace the importance of the alternative to the individual's life. So, again roughly and without suggesting that the calculation could actually be carried out, total liberty on the account I will develop can be thought of as:

$$\sum_{i=0}^{n} p_i \cdot v_i \cdot d_i$$

where p_i is the probability of the alternative, from 0 to 1, and v_i and d_i

are understood as above. So to fill in the account of personal freedom I will discuss the new and partially new factors: the number, variety, and value of the alternatives. Probability will also require some re-assessment in its new setting.

12. THE NUMBER AND VARIETY OF ALTERNATIVES

There is abundant evidence that people typically value having a wider range of alternatives for action. We hear frequent reference to "keeping one's options open." And at least part of the evil of restraint and coercion lies in the closing down of alternatives. Assuming rational management of decision costs,[3] we need never lose anything in having more alternatives, and we may gain something. In fact, in Chapter VII I will argue that something of value is *always* gained, when one gains a new alternative, even if the overall effect is a loss in value. But that contention is not essential for present purposes. I need not claim that the addition of a new alternative always increases freedom. If the new alternative turned out to be of no value at all, the v term would go to 0 and that alternative would contribute nothing to the individual's total freedom. Short of the $v = 0$ possibility, gaining an alternative is desirable for the individual and I shall, therefore, follow Berlin in taking it to increase the individual's total freedom.

Like Berlin, too, I am under no illusion that it is actually possible to count alternatives. It is typically arbitrary whether we take two slightly different ways of doing something as representing one alternative or two. We will not be able to assign cardinal numbers to different individuals' stocks of alternatives, and so, of course, the summation notation I made provisional use of last section cannot be taken literally.

It is worth noticing, however, that we can sometimes make ordinal comparisons with respect to alternatives. If A can do anything B can do and some more things besides, then A has more alternatives than B. And, of course, if I can do everything today I could do yesterday, plus something new, then I have more alternatives today than yesterday.[4] In some cases, we can make these ordinal judgments even where one set of alternatives is not a subset of the other. At the very least in extreme situations, say comparing the prisoner with the parolee, it is clear who has more alternatives. The ability to make these sorts of comparisons, especially that one has more or fewer alternatives today than yesterday, will, I think, be sufficient for ethics and political philosophy.

The counting problem for alternatives nearly compels recognition of the fact that the *variety* of the alternatives must be as relevant to freedom as is their number. The doubt is whether to count similar possible courses of action as different alternatives or variants of the same alternative. This problem does not arise with two alternatives which are very different from each other. Since very different alternatives must be counted separately and similar ones may either be counted as one or two, anyone who believes, with Berlin, that the number of alternatives is relevant to the extent of freedom must believe that their diversity is relevant as well.

It is independently plausible that, other things being equal, we add more to an individual's freedom when we open up a very different new alternative than when we open up a new alternative similar to alternatives the individual already has. If I am free to be a pitcher or a poet, I am freer than if my options are being a pitcher or a shortstop.

There are no objective standards for this sort of "degree of difference." As a first approximation, we should take as the standard the degree of difference among alternatives as judged by the individual in question. Since we are concerned about the value of freedom for the individual, the appropriate measure of degree of difference is, for the most part, the individual's own. In fact, it is probably best to think of the individual as making an intuitive range of alternatives judgment; where range embraces both difference and number.

There are, however, some minor problems in taking the individual's judgment of the range of alternatives as definitive. We do not want to count the individual's range of alternatives as very great simply because the individual lacks, or has been prevented from developing, an imagination sufficiently powerful to provide an appropriate comparison class for the alternatives he or she actually has. Even when alternatives are imaginable, one may mistake their degree of difference in a straightforward way. When things are actually encountered, we often feel that they were either more foreign or less foreign to our previous experience than we had expected them to be. We simply lack evidence when we estimate the degree of difference of unexperienced alternatives. These problems in relying simply and directly on the individual's own sense of the range of alternatives loom somewhat larger if we imagine a dictator who, through clever propaganda, makes the few and similar options provided seem to represent a considerable range of difference, while the forbidden options seem to differ but little from the options provided. What we want to say in this case is that the victims of such propaganda are less free than they believe themselves to be. The way to get this result, while still keeping some hold on the individual as the measure of the range of alternatives, is probably to turn to an idealization of the individual. For example, we might take as definitive the degree of difference the individual would judge there to be between two alternatives if he or she had tried both of them. Unfortunately, this counter-factual needs to be further filled in, and complexities abound. For present purposes, it will have to suffice to be aware of these problems.

Let me now mention a few consequences of taking an individual's total freedom to depend on the number and variety of his or her alternatives. In the first place, it follows that personal freedom does not have an upper bound. Finite beings will always lack some logically possible alternatives. So, in principle, we can always increase anyone's freedom.[5] This does not preclude us from talking about an individual as being "free." After all, we talk about things' being large. What we intend by a "free" individual may vary somewhat with context, but it will always be someone who has a relatively high degree of total freedom relative to the conversation's background, either actual or assumed.

While freedom has no upper bound, it does have a lower bound – no alternatives. Someone who is unconscious will, for example, have no alternatives and no freedom at that moment. (This is significant in showing that a lack of freedom is not always undesirable; at least if it is temporary.)

I am somewhat tempted to say that an individual who has but one alternative is also unfree, though that would run against the spirit of my account as represented in the last section. Moreover, it is slightly awkward to say that someone is totally unfree who is free to do something. In fact, of course, the counting problem makes the possibility of a single alternative entirely academic. Short of extreme science fiction situations, we can always find several (very similar) alternatives where we can find one. The intuition that an individual who has but one alternative is unfree is, then, better expressed by saying that one who has a very narrow range of alternatives is not very free.

The most controversial element of a view on which the extent of one's freedom depends on the range of one's alternatives is its "positive" implications. Let me own up at once to what is perhaps the most alarming sort of example. Since I cannot fly like an eagle, I am less free than I would be if I could. I know that some people will regard this as an outlandish thing to say. Insofar as it is so regarded because of considerations of "ordinary language," or because it is thought to result from, or in, conceptual confusions, I will try to answer the objections in Chapter VI. It may also be regarded as outlandish because it is of no interest to political philosophy that I cannot fly like an eagle. With this objection I am in entire agreement, as a matter of political philosophy. It is "social liberty," not "personal freedom," that is of direct interest to political philosophy, and my social liberty, as will be explained shortly, is not diminished by the fact that I cannot fly like an eagle.

Suppose, for the moment, that I can make good on my promissory notes, and nothing horrible happens if we count someone as less free because he or she cannot do the physically impossible. There is still the question what is to be gained by characterizing freedom in this way. Recall that my guiding principle is to define freedom so that it reflects what is valuable for the individual about freedom – or within what we intuitively think of as the "freedom neighborhood." In this light, the question is whether physically impossible alternatives would ever be valuable to have, if only that were possible. The answer to this question is clearly in the affirmative. My not being able to fly like an eagle is something I have, from time to time, had reason to regret. And while we certainly do not benefit from everything about technological progress, we do typically benefit by the alternatives opened up by the retreat of physical impossibility.

Moreover, most negative libertarians would grant that I am now free to eat breakfast in Paris and supper in Seattle on the same day, while no one was free to do this a century ago. It is certainly natural to say that I have more freedom in this respect than did my ancestors. People *do* say this sort of thing. And while liberation through technology may be an over-worked cliche, which ignores the other side of the coin, it has, like most cliches, an element of truth. If, then, we grant that an enlargement of what is physically possible expands freedom, we must say that I was, other things equal, less free before the expansion. And, of course, if the expansion does not take place (even if it *cannot* take place), I am less free than I would be if it were to take place. This, of course, is just the positive thesis.

The following case represents another approach to the motivation behind the positive account. Suppose that A cannot see because of a congenital disorder of the optic nerve, while B is locked into a permanent blindfold by order of the king. Politically, there is a great difference between these two cases. But it would make no real difference to me whether I was the victim of the one or the other of these misfortunes, so long as neither provided any hope of being overcome. So, as a matter of personal freedom, I take both these conditions to restrict freedom equally.

Similarly, a person A trapped in a cave by a spontaneous rock fall may have just about the same alternatives as someone B locked in a prison. A, I think, would not be much cheered by the negative libertarian's assurance that, since deliberate human intervention was not involved, A did not lose any freedom when the entrance to the cave became blocked. A is, for the negative account, freer, or at least less unfree, than B, though B can do everything A can. Again, it is because the limitation on A's actions are just as undesirable as those on B's actions, that I take A as well as B to have little total freedom.

13. THE PROBABILITY OF ALTERNATIVES

When we were concerned with the degree of freedom to perform a particular action in Section 7, it seemed as if the probability factor should be understood as varying with the context. For example, in certain contexts what seems relevant is the agent's own estimate of the probabilities, while in other contexts some more objective notion of probability is required. Similarly, in some contexts a low probability of success seems to count more against the freedom to do something than it does in other contexts. Since my present purpose is to put together an account of the agent's total freedom, embracing all his or her alternatives, it will not do to apply different procedures for assigning probability to those various alternatives. Interpersonal and even intrapersonal comparisons of freedom require a uniform procedure for assigning probabilities.

Following the general strategy of defining freedom in a way sensitive to what is valuable about freedom for the individual, there is an initial temptation to settle on subjective agent probabilities for the definition of total freedom. There are certainly purposes for which this is the appropriate course. How much freedom someone, or some class of people, perceive themselves to have is often a matter of considerable importance. If I think it is very improbable that I could succeed at x, I will usually not try x. It is, however, very unintuitive to say that I really am exactly as free as I think I am. To return to an old theme, the prisoner who deludedly fancies himself a new Houdini is not free to walk out of his cell.

In Section 7, I suggested that agent probability, restricted by a reasonableness requirement, is appropriate in many contexts where we are concerned with the freedom to do a particular thing. Might it prove a satisfactory standard of probability for total freedom as well? It avoids the problem of the pseudo-Houdini. It does, of course, require the use of a fictitious "reasonable estimator of probability" when the actual agent is not reasonable. And there are important difficulties about how this fiction is to be defined. But these difficulties are shared with other uses of the "reasonable man" test and are probably not insuperable. We do know the evidence that the reasonable estimator has to go on. It is just the evidence that the actual agent has.

My chief objection to adopting reasonable agent probability for the characterization of total personal freedom is the following. I would want to allow the possibility that a social critic should be right in saying that people are less free than they believe themselves to be because they hold false, though reasonable, estimates of the probabilities of certain alternatives.

Suppose that, as the result of a sophisticated education-propaganda system, most people believe, quite reasonably, that it is highly probable that they would become rich and powerful if only they chose to apply themselves and work hard. This social myth is in large part responsible for people's belief that they and their society have a great deal of freedom. Through diligent research, Karl discovers that this widespread social belief is false. For most people, the probability of their achieving wealth and power would be quite low, however diligently they applied themselves to the task. Karl claims that people are less free than they think they are (and, of course, that this was true even before Karl discovered it). Assuming that Karl's research is correct, I would think that we ought to accept his conclusion about freedom as well. But to do so is to say that the probability estimates everyone had made, though reasonable, were not determinative of the extent of their freedom.

The standard of probability suggested by this case might be called probability on "the best possible theory." By "probability on the best possible theory" I mean the best probability estimate that human beings could come up with using the best possible procedures. (This is not necessarily equivalent to the "fundamental probabilities" as they would appear to an omniscient observer.[6] There may well be limits to the best possible science, especially the best possible social science.)

Unfortunately, probability on the best possible theory also has problems as a standard for total freedom. It is *too* objective, as is shown by the "believable bluff" case. Suppose that A points a gun at B and demands B's life savings. As it turns out, A's "gun" is a stage prop which can fire only blanks, though it looks exactly like a real .38. We do not want to count, as making a large contribution to freedom, B's alternative of defying the threat and keeping the money, since B quite reasonably believes that such an action would be fatal. Suppose, however, that if B were a highly trained psychologist, specially versed in criminal behavior, B could discern, through subtle cues, that A was bluffing and that the gun must be a fake. Such a psychologist, then, would come up with a very different estimate of the probability of refusing to hand over the money and living to spend it than would our original B. But to adopt the psychologist's estimate of the probability, and thus of freedom, rather than B's own would be very unintuitive. We do think that believable bluffs coerce non-experts, even if an expert could tell it was a bluff. I conclude, then, that the "best possible theory" standard is not acceptable for our purposes as it stands. My proposal is to use a combination of the "reasonable agent" standard and the "best possible theory" standard as follows:[7]

(1) If A uses or is disposed to use A's own estimate of the probability of doing x in deciding whether to attempt x (or to do some action which

might foreseeably result in A's doing x), and if a low probability of doing x tends to discourage A, then assign the alternative of doing x the lower of the "reasonable agent" and "best possible theory" probabilities.

(2) Otherwise assign the alternative of doing x the "best possible theory" probability.

The basic idea behind this proposal is first that one is never made freer by virtue of mistakenly thinking that the probabilities of one's actions are higher than they would be on a more objective standard. Second, one may be made less free by virtue of thinking that the probabilities of one's actions are lower than they would be on a more objective standard, insofar as so thinking tends to affect one's decisions negatively.

So in Karl's society, people would be less free than they took themselves to be (assuming they made no compensating mistakes with respect to the other variables of freedom). And in the coercive bluff case, the victim is not counted as free to a high degree to refuse to hand over the money, even though an expert in the same situation would have been.

The reason for clause (2) emerges from the following sort of case. Lana believes reasonably that it is impossible for her to jump 25 feet. After many years of work and first class coaching, her performance has "plateaued out" at about 22′. However, since that is a respectable distance and one which places Lana well in meets, she is no more deterred from jumping by her belief that she will never make 25′ than she is by her inability to jump 100′. One day, Lana surprises herself by jumping 25′1″. Clause (2) prevents the unintuitive result that Lana does something she was unfree to do (or, what amounts to the same thing, that Lana does something the alternative of doing which contributed nothing to her freedom).

The desired result could be achieved in this case without clause (2); that is, on a procedure that *always* takes the lower of the reasonable agent and best possible theory probabilities. All we have to do is add the following independently plausible proviso: If it is logically possible for A to do x, then any probability measure on which the probability of A's doing x is 0 is unreasonable. (There is always some very small chance that the laws of nature will suddenly change.) But while the simpler procedure, with the addition of this proviso, would take care of the case as stated, it would not do so if Lana thought her probability of jumping 25′ was non-zero, but exceedingly low. In such cases, it seems intuitive to say that Lana was freer than she reasonably thought herself to be. Hence, the necessity for clause (2) to properly cover those cases where the agent's own probability estimates do not negatively affect the agent's decisions.

With clause (2) in place, the first clause becomes somewhat complex,

but the whole procedure is still surprisingly simple against the background
of the large number of approaches to probability that are, I suspect,
relevant to the freedom to do a particular thing in various contexts. It is
bound to introduce some complexity and conflict with intuition when we
give up the luxury of tailoring the probability treatment to the context in
order to produce a uniform standard for "computing" total freedom. But
so far as I can see, the two-part procedure stated above gives intuitive
results in a wide range of cases while avoiding any major difficulties.

14. THE VALUE OF ALTERNATIVES

I intend to include under this heading both Berlin's category (c), importance to the agent's life plan, and his category (e), value for the agent and
(possibly) for the society. I will first consider value and importance purely
from the agent's perspective, and later consider whether the value for the
society ought to be brought in.

I take value and importance together because importance to the
individual is one sort of value. What is important to my life-plan is more
valuable to me than what is irrelevant to or incompatible with my
life-plan. And it is, I think, intuitive that this sort of value makes a
difference in the extent of my freedom. If tomorrow I lose an alternative
on which I had decided and which was necessary for other goals to which
I was committed, my freedom is diminished more than it would be by a
law against flagpole sitting.

Centrality to a life-plan is, however, not the only feature of an
alternative that gives it more weight with respect to freedom. That I have
decided on an alternative or am seriously considering it, surely gives it
some status, even if it is not part of my life-plan in any sense more
exalted than that I have chosen it or might choose it. (I suppose that a
great deal that we do does not have anything to do with our life-plans.)
An alternative that I am not considering may have more or less status
depending on whether I have rejected it or not, or whether or not I would
reject it if I happened to consider it. Even rejected alternatives should be
graded at least as to the probability that they would be reconsidered
under various circumstances which might arise in the future.

Obviously, the value that the agent sees in the alternative will be
relevant at all these points. Consistency with the scheme set out in
Section 11 also requires giving special weight, under the present category,
to alternatives which the agent thinks valuable and would incorporate
into his or her life-plan, except that their probability is too low. These
alternatives will be given a heavy weight under the heading of value, but
will be cut down by the probability category. (If the probability is 0, then

the alternative's contribution to total freedom will also be 0, however valuable it is. This intuitive result corresponds to the "multiplicative" relation of the factors for each alternative.)

The general point of the value category, as it is, I think, for Berlin's categories (c) and (e), is to capture what was right in the long-held intuition of the negative tradition that freedom is somehow a matter of what the agent wants to do. Value represents a generalization of "what the agent wants to do." Bringing it in as a weight on alternatives making up the agent's total freedom allows us to retain the intuition while avoiding all the problems discussed in Section 10. Of course, the present account will not avoid all difficulties and controversy. Let me now turn to a few of the harder questions that arise with respect to the category of value.

It might be wondered whether we ought to accept as significantly contributing to liberty each and every (probable) alternative that the agent considers valuable, however odd the agent may be in thinking it valuable. We do not, at least for all purposes, honor the agent's assessment of probabilities. Why should we automatically honor his or her assessment of values? Of course, I have set as a guiding desideratum that personal freedom correspond to what is valuable about freedom for the individual. And it is natural in these terms to give the individual's own values the central place, even if they are idiosyncratic. But while natural, this is not entailed by the desideratum, at least if it is stated in terms of what *is* valuable *for* the agent, rather than what *seems* valuable *to* the agent.

If there is an objective standard of value such that 'alternative x is valuable for A' is routinely simultaneously true with 'A believes alternative x is not valuable for A,' then we could, perhaps, work out an account on which the value weighting of the alternatives would have very little to do with what the agent thinks is valuable. Quite independently of the difficulties of a value system which leaves what the agent values out of account, this suggestion does not seem to me a plausible one. We might criticize the excellence of people's lives by noting the divergence between their values and the true values, but to say that the content of their freedom is a matter of the true values rather than their own values opens the door for the kind of authoritarianism that any decent account of freedom must reject. Perhaps the individual must sometimes be willing to sacrifice his or her own plans in the name of higher values, but this is a sacrifice of freedom to other values, rather than a fulfillment of freedom. For these reasons, then, I would not reduce the weight of an alternative which the agent takes to be valuable, merely because it is an odd evaluation.

It is somewhat more plausible, however, that we might give some extra

weight, following Berlin, to those alternatives which "the general sentiment of the society" finds valuable. There is at least one "individualistic"
reason to do this. If the agent does not currently find the alternative
valuable, but most other people do, then that is some reason to believe
that the agent might change his or her mind about the alternative in the
future. On the other hand, if everyone in the history of humankind has
always regarded an alternative as odious, that makes it less likely that I
will come to find it attractive next week. But this consideration is already
built in directly, since added weight is given to those alternatives that the
agent has some likelihood of taking seriously in the future.

Presumably, Berlin has a different and more "intrinsic" reason for
wanting to take the public value system into account. I suppose the basic
idea is that we intuitively think of someone as having more freedom, if his
or her alternatives include several that are valuable on the public consensus. Suppose that we hear that Mason has alternatives which seem to the
public value system to be trivial, though some might be useful – for
example, collecting tolls on a bridge or collecting garbage. Nat has
alternatives each of which a large number of people regard as especially
valuable, including, say, composing symphonies and playing the concert
piano. I feel the attraction, under these circumstances, of saying that Nat
has more total freedom than Mason. But I think this attraction can easily
be explained without embracing Berlin's position. In the first place, we
are likely to think that Nat has all Mason's opportunities as well as those
mentioned for Nat. Having extra talents typically increases one's alternatives. If we imagine a case in which this isn't true, however, there will still
be an easy explanation of the intuition that Nat has more total freedom
than Mason. We assume with good inductive justification that Nat places
a higher value on composing and piano playing than Mason does on toll
and garbage collecting. If I discovered that Nat was bored or repulsed at
the idea of composing symphonies or playing the piano (and would
continue to be), while Mason was ecstatic at the thought of collecting tolls
or garbage (and would continue to be), then I would change my judgment
of their respective degrees of freedom. It is true that I take composing
symphonies (if they are decent) to represent a higher value than collecting
tolls, but I can express that in terms directly of the excellence of these
activities rather than putting it in terms of freedom.

For these reasons, my tendency is to think that Berlin is entirely wrong
in taking the public values to affect the extent of the individual's freedom.
I must admit, however, that I am not entirely certain about this point,
especially when it comes to certain extreme cases. It is not, in any event, a
central thesis of my account. (Indeed, it may seem ironic that I endorse,
here, a position more "individualistic" than Berlin's, given the politics of
the debate between positive and negative libertarians. The "left" or

"collectivist" side of positive libertarianism, however, does not arise from any deflation of the significance of the individual, but from its perception of the policy implications of taking each person's individuality seriously.)

If it turns out that I am wrong and Berlin right on this point, or if both of us are wrong and it is not the public values but the *true* values that affect liberty, it would be easy to bring that fact within the framework of the present account. In fact, one could construe the value category in any number of different ways, and still preserve the basic idea of the positive account. If, for example, one had strong perfectionist leanings and wanted to characterize freedom along those lines, one might take anything less than "worthwhile" or "excellent" actions to have no value. Under this treatment, the agent would not gain in freedom by gaining trivial alternatives. This is not the way I would treat trivial alternatives, but one might treat them in this way within a positive account of freedom.

My own view is that, for purposes of total freedom, the value category ought never to be taken to go to zero. Part of the reason for this is that it seems unintuitive to say that gaining an alternative (without losing any alternatives or changing the probability or value of the prior alternatives) does not increase the agent's freedom at all. It is even less intuitive to say that one has no liberty when one has several alternatives to choose among, all of which are at least slightly undesirable. This may sometimes be a particularly important kind of freedom. My stipulation that the value term not go to zero distinguishes this term from our ordinary notions of value, since we ordinarily do think that some things are of no value or even negative value. In partial defense of the stipulation, however, notice that it is less clear that an alternative can be of no value or negative value than that an object or action can be of no value or negative value.

Still, as I understand the value category of the analysis, it is somewhat different from other things we call "value." In fact, I call it "value" only because that word seems to carry more nearly the right associations than any other familiar word or short phrase. Moreover, it has a salutary vagueness. But I do bend the word somewhat to cover the rather disparate group of considerations that I intend. The central place in that group goes to the agent's plans, decisions, and desires, but there is room, as well, for plans and desires which the agent may come to have. Probably we should also include certain "counterfactual desires" – what *A* would desire if only, for example, *A* knew facts that *A*, in fact, is ignorant of, or what *A* would desire if only *A* had thought about the matter more carefully.

Even without including these counterfactual desires, the "value" category would not be unitary. Its various components may pull in different directions. For example, we sometimes decide to do things we know sit poorly with our life plans. So far as I can see, there is nothing that "integrates" the different components of the value category. So the overall judgment of value, for these purposes, will have to consist in an intuitionistic "weighing" of different considerations. (I must admit that this conclusion makes me nervous, since I am unsure that there can ultimately be anything but naked, arbitrary choice behind the "weighing" metaphor. Treatments of the value category other than the one I suggest, for example the perfectionist option mentioned above, may possibly be able to avoid this element of intuitionism, though I doubt that they can. And if they do, it will be at a price elsewhere.)

With the value category joining the number, variety, and probability of the alternatives, we complete the factors entering into the extent of an individual's total personal freedom. This notion of freedom will be relevant to a wide range of ethical issues, but to fit it to the purposes of political philosophy, it needs some slight alteration, to which I now turn.

CHAPTER V

SOCIAL LIBERTY

Since people very rarely live in isolation, the value of individual freedom must find its place in a social setting. The maximization, or even the protection, of positive personal freedom quickly becomes a political issue. So it is necessary, in continuing the analysis, to shift from the purely individual perspective and consider positive liberty as a social and political ideal.

I am going to call the version of freedom I propose for political analysis "social liberty." This is in preference to "political liberty" even though some political philosophers have used the latter phrase for roughly the phenomenon I will be concerned with. I do this because "political liberty" is often used in a narrower sense to refer to those liberties on which the political process depends in order to function properly. For example, democracy, in order to function in the spirit of its own rationale, is said to require a fairly broad range of liberties. (Some refer to these as "the political liberties," a phrase less liable to cause confusion than "political liberty.") A second use of "political liberty" makes it a synonym of "legal liberty." This is, again, too narrow for present purposes. No one believes that legal constraints are the only constraints of interest to political philosophy.

"Social liberty" no doubt has some misleading associations of its own, but I think it has usually been used, if vaguely, for personal freedom insofar as it is of interest to political philosophy. In any event, this is the way I intend to use that phrase. Social liberty, so understood, is still in the first instance something belonging to individuals. What is social about it is that society can increase or diminish it. For this reason it properly appears as part of a social or political ideal.

15. THE CHARACTERIZATION

It would be possible simply to use "personal freedom" unmodified for purposes of political philosophy. It is of political interest how much personal freedom there is in a given society, how it is distributed, how it might be increased, and how it compares with the level and distribution of personal freedom in other societies. But there is an aspect of personal freedom, as I have characterized it, that is irrelevant to political philosophy. This, as previously mentioned, is the fact that such impossibilities as flying like an eagle are counted among the things I am personally unfree to do. However, since I am not unfree to do such things as the result of social circumstances, we can omit these impossible alternatives from the purview of social liberty.

If freedom were never a matter of degree, the characterization could be made as follows:

(1) A is socially free to do x if and only if A is personally free to do x.
(2) A is socially unfree to do x if and only if both A is personally unfree to do x and A would be personally free to do x on some other possible social arrangement.

Under this definition, I am neither socially free nor socially unfree to fly like an eagle. This "gap" can be slightly awkward, but it is plausible enough, since flying like an eagle is not a social or political issue.

Notice that there is still a substantial positive component of social liberty under this preliminary characterization. Many incapacities – physical, intellectual, artistic, and so on – could be eliminated under favorable social arrangements. There are, I am sure, quite a few cripples who could run if there were sufficient social commitment to their rehabilitation. Following this characterization, all such cases are recognized as instances of social unfreedom, contrary to the negative conception.

Now let me modify the above characterization to take degrees of liberty into account:

(1) If A would be personally unfree to do x under all possible social arrangements, then the degree e of A's social liberty to do x is undefined.
(2) Otherwise, if A is personally free to degree d to do x, then e is the result of recomputing d leaving out of account anything which lowers the probability of x on every possible social arrangement. (If A is socially free to degree 0 to do x, then A is socially unfree to do x.)

Let me give an example of the operation of this formulation. Technical rock-climbing pitches are rated according to ascending difficulty: 4, 5.0, 5.1, ... 5.9, 5.10. In the actual world, with its social arrangement, the probability of my climbing a 5.10 pitch is perhaps non-zero, but it is very small. So, despite the high value I would place on it, this alternative contributes little to my personal freedom. However, on *any* possible social rearrangement, it would still be very improbable that I should climb a 5.10 pitch. The reason for this improbability is my lack of natural talent. Clause (2) instructs us to disregard this consideration, since it leads to a low probability on every possible social arrangement. In this case, this means recomputing my freedom to climb a 5.10 pitch on the supposition that I had the talent to do so. On this supposition the probability is very high that I would, if I tried, make the climb. The result is that I am socially free (to a high degree) to climb a 5.10 pitch.

By virtue of clause (1), the characterization shares with the preliminary version the feature of having "gaps" for such impossibilities as flying like an eagle. I am neither socially free nor socially unfree to do so. In a manner of speaking, clause (2) generalizes the effect of clause (1) in limiting what is counted as social unfreedom. My social freedom is greater than my personal freedom because not everything which limits my personal freedom is a product of social arrangements.

Again let me say that these modest complexities of characterization are not really necessary. "Personal freedom" as discussed last chapter could serve perfectly well in the social setting, unmodified. Comparisons of the freedom of individuals within a single society or between societies would be unaffected by those things everyone is unfree to do in every society.

My reason for characterizing two notions of liberty rather than one is that my chief purpose is, again, to persuade the negative libertarian of the value of a positive account. Negative libertians have traditionally found it unpalatable to count strictly impossible alternatives among the social unfreedoms. So, in a spirit of compromise, and at some cost to simplicity, I have characterized social liberty so that one is never socially less free by virtue of limitations which would exist under every social arrangement.

The account of social liberty I end up with sounds very much like what Berlin is talking about when he takes the absence of freedom to be "the closing of such doors or failure to open them, as a result, intended or unintended, of alterable human practices."[1] I have no disagreement with this formulation. It shows, again, how close Berlin sometimes comes to what I call a positive account of liberty. But, as usual, there are other passages which carry a much more traditionally negative message.

The fundamental sense of freedom is freedom from chains, from imprisonment, from enslavement by others. The rest is extension of this sense, or else metaphor . . . Freedom, at least in its political sense, is co-terminous with the absence of bullying or domination.[2]

It is hard for me to see that Berlin is consistent on this point. Surely not all alterable human failures to open doors are cases of bullying. After all, it is often through neglect that opportunities fail to be created for the disadvantaged. It is initially more plausible that all failures to open doors are the result of domination in some sense or other. A ruling class which neglects to provide decent education for the lower classes can justly be accused of keeping doors closed as the result of their domination. But there will be some alternatives which are not open even to members of the dominant class, which could be opened up, at least for a few, by social rearrangement. Surely these do not count as doors closed by domination. So Berlin's two characterizations are incompatible.

I think we can conclude from category (d) of Berlin's most detailed characterization of the extent of liberty, as well as from other explicit remarks,[3] that his real view is closer to the "bullying and domination" formulation than to the "alterable human practices" formulation. In exploring below some of the social policy consequences of the positive "alterable practices" characterization, it should become clearer why Berlin and the negative tradition would not embrace it.

Before looking at those policy consequences, let me call attention to an aspect of the "logic" of social freedom as I characterize it. In view of the scarcity of resources, there will always be people who, under different social circumstances, could do things which they cannot now do. For example, the development of capacities is frequently an expensive proposition. For this reason, as well as others, we can be sure that no society will develop all the capacities of its citizens. Social unfreedom can be shifted around, but it can never be entirely eliminated.

A too quick reading of the last conclusion might lead one to believe that social unfreedom, as characterized, becomes, by virtue of its inevitability, a useless category for social criticism. But the fact that every society will have some unfreedom does not, of course, entail that each society will have the same amount of unfreedom as every other society. And a society may not have a maximum amount of social freedom given its resources or even given its resources and its other value commitments. These facts suffice for social liberty to be a useful category of political criticism.

Finally, let me emphasize, as an introduction to the discussion of positive libertarian social policy, a major point of disagreement between the present analysis and traditional accounts of social liberty. No one would doubt that it is impermissible to pass and enforce a law requiring an (innocent) individual to wear a blindfold in everyday life. I contend, as will be discussed in detail later, that it is equally a blot against social liberty to permit a blind person, curable with a moderate expenditure, to go uncured.

16. OUTLINES OF A POSITIVE LIBERTARIAN SOCIAL PROGRAM

Obviously, a social program guided by considerations of positive liberty will seek to increase the number, diversity, desirability, and probability of alternatives available to the members of the society. This involves in the first place an elimination of most legal restrictions and personal interferences traditionally opposed by negative libertarians. In fact, I think the liberal tradition has frequently been too soft in its opposition to restrictions and interferences, even of the general sort it recognizes as liberty infringing. For example, relatively few negative libertarians have taken a stand against the legal restrictions on defamation and advocacy of crime. Even if these laws are socially beneficial, it is not at all clear to me that society ought to be permitted to restrict the individual's speech in these ways.

The largest difference between traditional libertarian views and positive libertarianism is, however, the latter's support for affirmative (and probably expensive) programs aimed at the development of human capacities, the provision of free time, and the supply of the equipment, facilities, and other means to the enlargement of life's possibilities.

The provision of ample free time is likely to be one of the costliest planks in the positive libertarian platform. It does, however, follow fairly directly from the general perspective of positive libertarianism. There are a great many alternatives which people find desirable and which cannot be explored while one is earning a living. This is not to say that useful and gainful labor is an evil to be eliminated where possible. But in an ideally free situation, all labor would be purely voluntary. If income and privileges were dispensed independently of whether one worked or how much one worked, then people could exercise full control of their own time. They would be free to follow whatever alternatives they chose. No doubt people would still choose to do some useful labor. Much work is, or can be made to be, intrinsically satisfying. But obviously much work cannot be. It is revealing, I think, that many nineteenth century liberals found it no mark against liberty that factory workers or miners spent most of their waking hours at jobs which they hated. The sense in which these workers were doing what they "wanted" to do is a pretty thin sense.

In the real world of the foreseeable future, there will probably have to be some compromise with the ideal of complete control of one's own time through a voluntary labor system. Unless there is enough labor, other parts of the positive libertarian program will suffer, such as the development of capacities and the provision of facilities, equipment and the like. Other social goods would, of course, also suffer. It should be possible, however, to shorten the work day, the work week, and the work year without giving up too much on other fronts, at least in advanced industrial societies.

The important point is that capacities and the material prerequisites of freedom are not of value without the time to use them. Moreover, a wide range of activities require relatively little in the way of material support.

For this reason, a society might maximize liberty by requiring a fairly small amount of labor in exchange for a moderate standard of living. Perhaps those whose interests were in directions requiring less free time but more material support ought to be able to work longer hours for additional wages. The exact way of dealing with the trade-off between free time and material prosperity is something that must be worked out in the concrete in a given society. A positive libertarian program in the abstract can only emphasize the importance of free time to liberty and the desirability of at least a sufficient income to get along, even if one does not work or works only a minimum number of hours.

As already suggested, a society concerned with positive liberty would also give high priority to rehabilitation, education, training, and, in general, to those programs which remove incapacities and develop capacities. When our powers are undeveloped, we have relatively little freedom, even if we have plentiful free time and few interferences. The recent trend towards training narrowly restricted to qualifying one for a job or improving one's job performance is a development in nearly complete antithesis to the emancipatory role of education.

To enlarge alternatives available to people, it is also necessary to insure the availability of materials, instruments, facilities, and the like which people require to pursue their chosen activities, whether they be scientific, artistic, athletic, philosophic, religious or simply those of entertainment and amusement. The burgeoning of possibilities and pursuits in this century has been, in large part, the result of the development of technology. Technology has both opened new fields, like radio astronomy, and opened old fields to larger numbers through the mass production of such things as phonograph records, musical instruments, and small sailboats.

Some sorts of things, of course, cannot be made available for the sole use of every individual who would like to use them, for example, ocean-going yachts. Whatever the level of technological and industrial advancement, there will always be some things in this category. Both the expansion of liberty and considerations of justice require that these scarce objects be shared around widely rather than monopolized and underutilized by a small, privileged group as is typical today.

A society concerned about positive liberty will encourage diversity among its citizens. The main current of negative libertianism, by contrast, would protect diversity, but not encourage it. (Mill is an exception to this rule, but his enthusiasm for diversity for its own sake seems, at points, to outrun both his negative account of liberty and his utilitarianism.) There are, of course, certain tendencies in human society and social dynamics which favour the development of diversity. But there are also powerful tendencies towards uniformity, only some of which are checked by laws protecting non-conformists from outside interference. Therefore, since diversity widens the available alternatives, the proper social policy is to encourage as well as protect it.

In particular, it is desirable that a wide range of various theories on controversial subjects be made available in the schools and to the public at large. This may sometimes involve a special effort to seek out, develop, and subsidize the publication of offbeat and unpopular ideas. Some particular mechanisms for accomplishing this will be taken up shortly.

The encouragement of diversity ought to extend to some level of subsidization for those who experiment with new life styles and modes of community organization. The alternatives such experiments open up add, not only to the liberty of their participants, but, to greater or lesser degree, to the liberty of each of us. If their way seems appealing in practice, we can join or copy them.

In part for these same reasons, groups should be allowed, though not necessarily encouraged, to secede from the political society altogether, perhaps taking with them a portion of land and other resources proportional to their numbers.[4] In the seceded community, they ought to be able to live by their own lights and laws, however different or silly.

This policy would have to be shored up by various protections both of the larger society and of individuals in the seceded society. The two chief principles are mentioned by Mill. Separated communities ought not to be interfered with "provided they commit no aggression on other nations, and allow perfect freedom of departure to those who are dissatisfied with their ways."[5] Some additional restrictions may be required to prevent the most extreme forms of indoctrination, especially of the young.

17. A POSITIVE APPROACH TO SPEECH

As suggested above, a positive approach to liberty requires the encouragement, rather than simply the protection, of diversity. Diversity increases available alternatives. With regard to speech this means insuring a reasonably wide hearing for a range of ideas – profound and silly, plausible and harebrained, uplifting and degrading.

Some ideas are naturally powerful and spread by their own dynamic. They appeal either to the rich or the powerful or teachers, or they have a direct and dramatic appeal to large numbers of people. Depending on the social and historical setting, such self-starting ideas may make up a fairly diverse group. So the (negative) protection of speech, if pursued rigorously enough, will often achieve commendable results. But some ideas have none of the above advantages. In fact, as is well known, beliefs that turned out to be both true and important often began their careers with few and powerless friends. The same can be said of ideas that proved false, but were plausible and worth considering.

There are various mechanisms for widening the range of ideas in the public arena. Mill proposed, for example, that "if opponents of all important truths do not exist, it is indispensable to imagine them, and supply them with the strongest arguments which the most skillful devil's advocate can conjure up."[6] The instruction that we are to "imagine" the dissenters leaves it a little unclear to what extent Mill is encouraging thought experiments in devil's advocacy and to what extent he would favor the establishment of institutions of devil's advocacy' perhaps socially funded. In any event, it seems that hiring devil's advocates, who would devote themselves full time to puncturing established doctrines and dreaming up plausible alternatives, would be an effective way of expanding the range of public discussion. Academic institutions in the West encourage a certain amount of devil's advocacy. But there could be a great deal more of it, and it could be brought more into the public arena. A devil's advocate cloistered away among specialists makes little contribution to the range of diversity of socially available ideas.

Another mechanism for promoting diversity in expression is the subsidized publication of ideas which would not otherwise receive publication. Of course, it would usually be financially unfeasible to publish every belief and theory, or even those actually held by somebody in the community.

One compromise policy for subsidized publication came from Lenin who, prior to the Bolshevik phase of the Revolution, was concerned about the dominance of the Russian press by the rich. Lenin was more a libertarian than the accepted histories of either East or West would grant, but there is no doubt that his libertarianism was deeply flawed, not always in ways excusable by the historical contingencies. Despite this, Lenin's 1917 proposal on the press[7] deserves serious consideration from positive libertarians. Subsidized printing facilities were to go to various parties in proportion to their numerical strengths. A small group urging the establishment of theocracy might get a mimeograph to use, while major political parties would control daily newspapers. Obviously, this policy does not answer to all the needs of diversity, but it would militate against the domination of the press by special groups and give any group some access to an audience. It does this without an open-ended commitment to the publication of any idea that comes down the pike. Its major weakness is in failing to encourage friendless ideas of merit. But this is the task of devil's advocacy.

It will not go unnoticed by negative libertarians that the mechanisms for encouraging the publication of diverse ideas require money. This money will have to be diverted from other sources and could otherwise be available for individuals to use at their own discretion. It will be necessary to make some sacrifices elsewhere to insure a robust social exchange of ideas. Except in the very poorest of societies, these sacrifices are well worth it.

It might be wondered under what principles a devil's advocate would select theories to be pursued and, similarly, how positive libertarians would be guided in producing textbooks for schools which would reflect diverse points of view. Presumably, the principles of Section 12 would urge us to encourage the very wildest of unorthodox theories, since these will differ most from the accepted theories. But wildly unorthodox ideas will often be crazy or pernicious. Take the (contemporary) flat earth theory as an example of the former and racism as an example of the latter. When it comes to the encouragement (rather than the protection!) of such ideas, obviously, a certain balance has to be struck. In the first sort of case, a theory which is terribly implausible simply does not constitute much of an intellectual alternative. It fails under the "value" criteria of Section 14; interpreted in terms of such features as goodness of evidence. The second case, racist beliefs, have the same defect. In addition, they have the more serious defect that they encourage alternatives for action which are, from a social point of view, highly undesirable. The small contributions these alternatives make to individual freedom conflict with other important considerations of social policy, including considerations of liberty. In short, there are abundant good reasons to discourage racist behavior and, therefore, not to *encourage* racist ideas.

Obviously, this brief discussion falls far short of canvassing all the means of encouraging a diverse public exchange of ideas. There are also any number of interesting and difficult public policy issues raised by the general approach suggested here, but which I cannot go into. My chief point is that practical mechanisms for the encouragement of diversity in expression are possible, but have only rarely been championed by negative libertarians. This is remarkable since most of the consequentialist arguments for protecting dissident opinion apply equally well to the encouragement of dissident opinion. And many negative libertarians have made a great deal of these consequentialist arguments. This is, then, another point at which the logic of their position ought to push negative libertarians on to, at least a limited, positive libertarianism.

18. REDISTRIBUTION

In a society in which people hold very different amounts of wealth, the maximization of positive liberty would presumably involve some redistribution from rich to poor. Wealth tends to have a decreasing marginal efficiency in the production of (diverse, desirable) alternatives. When we give $10,000 to a poor person, it expands his or her horizons more than if we gave the same sum to a rich person. This sort of redistribution also appeals to our egalitarian intuitions. It runs counter, of course, to those theories on which property rights take precedence over considerations of positive liberty.

Another kind of redistribution, which has already been suggested, would shift resources so as to remove easily remedial incapacities and handicaps. $2,000 for an operation which enables someone to walk, talk, see or hear buys more in the way of increased alternatives than it would if used in almost any other way. A tax for such purposes again appeals to egalitarianism as well as to the concern for liberty.

Some transfers, however, which would be dictated if our sole guide to policy were the maximization of positive liberty, might conflict with our sense of fair equality of treatment. It may be, for example, that providing opportunities and alternatives for many physically and mentally handicapped persons costs more than similar increases in opportunities and alternatives for the non-handicapped. Sports for the physically handicapped, for example, often require expensive special equipment. Education for the mentally retarded requires a great deal of individual attention. Certain sorts of very elaborate medical procedures for correcting incapacities probably fall in this same category. It might be argued that we should maximize positive liberty by shifting resources *away* from the handicapped in these cases, in favor of the non-handicapped for whom expenditures go farther.

If the factual premises here are correct, which they must be in at least some cases, that seems a good reason to conclude that we must not simply maximize the social sum of positive liberty. Just because liberty is so important, it is unacceptably unfair for some people to have a great deal more of it than do others, even if this distribution arises as a result of maximizing total liberty. (This is just one of several sorts of cases where other values ought to serve as constraints upon the maximization of liberty.)

It is probably not possible to specify *a priori* just how far redistribution ought to go to equalize positive liberty. It is plausible, I think, that people who are handicapped ought to be brought up nearer the level of liberty of the rest of us by putting considerable resources at their disposal, even though this means a fairly heavy tax burden on the rest of us. The redistribution policy ought to take into account, however, people's general attitude toward it. If the policy is widely thought to be terribly demanding, and people live in fear of the next round of taxation, that would suggest that the redistribution may have gone too far. If, on the other hand, people are reassured by the fact that they will be the beneficiaries of considerable aid should they ever become seriously handicapped, the program will serve as a desirable, if expensive, form of social insurance. (Perhaps transfers should be restricted in cases where the handicaps are self-inflicted or the results of excessively risky activities.)

If we were in a Rawlsian choice situation – ignorant of who we would turn out to be in society – it seems clear that we would favor a redistributive policy of the general sort suggested above. We would want to insure that our range of alternatives would not be too limited. So we would approve the use of tax money to remedy otherwise irremediable incapacities. We would, I think, also approve transfers to all but the very rich who have wholly irremediable handicaps, as a form of compensation for those handicaps. And we would approve transfers from rich to poor, in partial equalization of the differences wealth makes in positive liberty.

I doubt that we could specify, in Rawlsian abstraction, the exact principles under which these redistributions ought to work. In particular, it is not obvious that we should follow a policy of maximizing the minimum level of positive liberty. Other considerations or principles might dictate a redistribution policy which does not maximize the minimum. Egalitarian concerns, on the one hand,[8] and problems with the rigorousness of this principle in practice, on the other, are among the likely contra-maximin considerations.

The fact that a general, if not a specific, policy of liberty-expending and liberty-equalizing redistributions would be chosen "behind a veil of ignorance" seems to me to be morally significant. A point of view which abstracts from our particular interests is a point of view which everyone falling under a morality could adopt. That we would choose a given principle or policy from this point of view gives it a special status. Perhaps, in fact, what we would choose from such a point of view *constitutes* (at least part of) the moral truth. In some matters, there may be nothing "higher than" such idealized human choices, or in any other respect better qualified to serve as the basis for moral truth. Even if this chastened version of moral subjectivism is incorrect, however, something like Rawls' "original position" is a plausible *test* of moral principles. It is a good reason for thinking that a principle is correct if it would be chosen behind a veil of ignorance, though that may not be the only sort of good moral reason, and the reasonableness of what is so chosen might be defeated by other moral arguments. Still, that a principle passes a Rawlsian test at least says something for its moral credentials, and the burden shifts to its opponents to show why it is objectionable.

It should be obvious from this chapter's discussion that the various component parts of a positive libertarian social program involve numerous possibilities for conflict among themselves. A given policy may add to liberty in one respect while diminishing it in another. The analysis of the structure of personal freedom given in Chapter IV provides a framework for discussing such conflicts but, at best, only a partial procedure for resolving them. It does not, for example, answer such questions as how many moderately desirable alternatives equal, in their contribution to liberty, one very desirable alternative. It is, presumably, just such questions that would arise in a debate over what material-intensive alternatives we are willing to give up to insure a given amount of free time for everyone.

That a positive libertarian social program does not automatically resolve all conflicts which arise within its framework is neither very surprising nor too much to be regretted. Such other social ideals as negative libertarianism have this same failing. The question when we may interfere with A to prevent A from interfering with B does not, for example, seem to have any satisfactory general answer. A great deal hinges, first, on the seriousness of A's interference with B and, second, on the seriousness of our preventative interference with A. The determination of seriousness of interference involves, in many cases, the same kind of intuitions as enter into assessments of the extent of positive liberty.

Moreover, as already suggested, the advancement of positive liberty is not, by itself, a satisfactory social ideal. A complete social ideal would have to take account of such diverse goods and moral requirements as justice, equality, happiness, the minimization of suffering, scientific and cultural achievement, community, and democratic participation – just to give a partial list. These values will sometimes conflict among themselves and with liberty. So even if positive liberty were itself a unitary ideal, that would only postpone the possibility of conflict a bit.

Conflicts between different values and moral principles, resolvable only on a case by case basis, seem to be a fact of life. It is a mark in favor of a moral theory if it eliminates or minimizes such cases by giving principles for adjudicating disputes and prioritizing conflicting values and principles. But this power in adjudication must not be bought at the cost of giving results which conflict in too many cases with our considered moral judgments, as is the tendency for such unitary moral theories as Utilitarianism.

In practice, the inability to settle all social conflicts is not such a serious liability for a social ideal. That people must look to their intuitions as well as to moral theory and the facts of the situation is no great handicap. So long as they place their decisions in the framework of a social ideal, and base them in part on that ideal, the social ideal is performing a useful function. If this much is true, it will be a worthwhile enterprise to propose, criticize, debate, and clarify social ideals.

19. LEFT AND RIGHT LIBERTARIANISM

The sort of libertarian social program just outlined is presumably incompatible with the existence of great private concentrations of economic power. The reason for this, simply put, is that positive liberty requires resources. It takes resources to give people a choice of what to do with their time – in particular, discretion (even limited) over how much they will work. It takes resources to remove or reduce incapacities and to develop powers and talents. It takes resources to provide the equipment and other means needed for many sorts of alternatives. Sufficient resources are likely to be channeled in these directions only through a conscious economic program. The chance of its happening as an unintended result of an economy organized around different goals is virtually nil. Obviously, private enterprise is animated by very different purposes. In particular, the motivations of private wealth and power and the profitability of the firm are at cross purposes with the sorts of redistributions and new institutions which would expand positive liberty under a constraint of reasonable equality.

To break the private concentrations of power, and to prevent the appearance of their functional equivalent in the form of bureaucratic power, is to extend democracy into the economy, from the shop floor and local union to the "commanding heights" of the financial system. Simultaneously, it will be necessary to diminish the influence that wealth has over the political process in the Western democracies through the financing of candidates and the shaping of public opinion. (Again, it is not necessary to ban the political views of the wealthy, but only to insure that they have abundant competition.)

The thoroughly democratic control of the economy at all levels is what I mean by "socialism." So "democratic socialism" is redundant. It is a redundancy, however, that is often useful given the popular identification of socialism with state ownership; an identification encouraged for different purposes by the orthodoxy of both West and East.

It would be possible for a democratic socialism to be non-libertarian. However, respect for human autonomy is the natural motivation for so radical and thorough-going a democracy. So it would be odd for its partisans not also to be concerned about liberty. But it is possible at least to imagine such a situation. I do not, then, claim that socialism *entails* a free society. I claim only that it is the most plausible institutional context for a free society.

In the so-called "socialist countries," the minority concentrations of power are not "private" in precisely the same sense as in the West. But the power centers are in many ways remarkably similar. In fact, the dynamics of the economies are also strikingly similar, despite their seeming differences.[9] In any event, it should be obvious that the monopoly of power held by bureaucrats, led by the upper levels of the communist parties, is the fundamental obstacle to socialism and liberty in the East. The prescription is the same – the institution of a thorough-going democracy at all levels of economic, political, and social life. Even if, contrary to fact, the Communist bureaucrats intended to preside over a system of positive liberty, they would not succeed. The top-down administration of liberty would be too distant and mechanical to be sufficiently responsive to the value dimensions of liberty. Moreover, there is a well known and powerful dynamic which tends to turn the altruism of any ruling group into its opposite.

I do not expect that these remarks will turn anti-socialists into socialists or persuade the friends of the American or Russian or Chinese regimes to abandon their sympathies. Arguments appropriate to the task of political conversion must usually be long and highly empirical. They ought also to be two-sided. You cannot really understand my politics, until you see the way I respond to yours. And if I wish to convert you, I ought also to give you the chance to convert me. Dialogue becomes even more important as we move from abstractions and the purity of social ideals into the empirical analysis of present systems and the practical issues of social change. For these reasons, the intent of this work is not conversion, though I do not think political conversion is unphilosophical. Political philosophy is properly partisan, but partisan political issues obviously outrun any essay in political philosophy. What I am trying to do is to clear some of the philosophical barriers to the acceptance of a "left" libertarianism. I will argue that the root theory of liberty underlying this political ideal is neither incoherent, nor confused, nor, more importantly, morally unsound. In fact, I hope to show that positive liberty has the proper moral credentials for centrality in a political philosophy.

Since what I am giving is a partial defense of left libertarianism, it may be useful, at this point, to summarize its differences with libertarianism of the right; the libertarianism of unrestricted private enterprise. Right libertarianism is little more a flourishing political movement than is left libertarianism. Politicians who support "free" enterprise also tend to support a large military budget, conscription, strong police methods, and laws against drugs, pornography and revolutionary organizations. Still, if not the philosophy of the practical political right, right libertarianism is often useful to these politicians and their supporters. Right libertarianism provides an articulated theory which can sometimes be made use of, and other times conveniently forgotten. Moreover, right libertarianism represents an intellectually attractive alternative to the often muddled and *ad hoc* politics of the middle of the road. As a result, right libertarianism is enjoying a modest intellectual popularity.

The chief point of dispute between left and right libertarianism is, obviously, their different conceptions of liberty. Right libertarians support the negative account of liberty. Thus, much of the argument of this essay can be read as a criticism of right libertarianism, though it applies, of course, to a considerably wider range of liberal positions. The right libertarian wants to minimize restraint and coercion, other things equal. The left libertarian wants to maximize the range of concrete alternatives for choice. This leads to wide differences with respect to health policies, educational policies and many other social questions.

Following from their different views on liberty, left and right libertarians disagree about equal liberty. Right libertarians reject inequalities in negative liberty. They oppose any society in which some are coerced or restrained by others except perhaps as necessary for punishment or out of considerations of serious incompetence. Slave and serf holding societies are impermissible. Left libertarians reject, in addition, large inequalities in concrete alternatives and opportunities. This means a rejection of any society in which there are considerable differences in wealth and power.

Of course, left libertarianism would (democratically) infringe some liberties which the right libertarian would protect. In particular, the liberty of private control over the economy or any of its larger units: banks, factories, railroads, large farms and the like. Also infringed would be the liberty to hold great concentrations of wealth in whatever form. These are doubtless liberties. Against these liberties, the left libertarian would raise barriers of restraint or coercion if necessary. The liberties in question are very significant for some people. It is unfortunate that the lives of the wealthy and powerful have to be interfered with, but it is necessary in order to expand overall liberty. Fortunately, the number of people for whom the liberties of large scale ownership are concrete is relatively small. Moreover, considerations of distributive justice deflect many of the complaints of the wealthy over the elimination of their prerogatives.

The left libertarian will also tend to doubt the stability of any society organized around right libertarian principles. Unrestricted private enterprise inevitably leads to great concentrations of wealth. Nearly as inevitably, this wealth is converted into political power which then intervenes, in a self-interested way, in the economy. Free enterprise becomes restricted in the interest of the wealthy. Instead of a minimal state, we end up with a state which interferes, restrains and coerces on a broad range of fronts. Against the impressive empirical evidence that wealth and economic power breed political power, the right libertarian has an uphill struggle to show that his or her social ideal is not, in practice, a self defeating one. I think that struggle is doomed to failure. If one is really committed to liberty – even negative liberty – one will have to abandon private enterprise.

Finally, there is obviously a difference between left and right libertarianism over the issue of democracy. For the left libertarian, extensive democracy is a morally proper means to liberty; indispensable in practice.

Moreover, democracy has a deeper justification in the same concern for individual autonomy that underlies the value of liberty. Right libertarians are, typically, either hostile to or at least uncomfortable with democracy, seeing it as a usurper of properly individual choices. At the extreme, they deny that democracy should play any role at all in a free society. But, as will be discussed in Section 34, no one with libertarian pretensions can support the minority imposition of a constitution. Therefore, I fail to see how the right libertarian can avoid granting some role to democracy in settling certain basic features of the society. Even if this is granted, however, there will still be plenty of room for disagreement over the proper role of democracy. For the left libertarian, that role is large in the elimination of oppressive private power and in the creation of a system of positive liberty.

It may be worth recalling, however, that there are points of contact between left and right libertarians. Both support the freedoms of speech, conscience and association (though the left libertarian would want to expand the traditional freedoms with positive mechanisms). Both would like to see the final decision be individual in such matters as what parts of the body must be garbed, who may express affection in public, what forms marriage may take, what movies we may send children to, what may be said on television, and how one may risk life and limb. Both would like to see greater individual choice over what substances one may inflict upon one's body. Both are opposed to bureaucratic power. These agreements are by no means unimportant, even if they are overshadowed by the differences about liberty and democracy which lead to their fundamental disagreement about private enterprise.

CHAPTER VI

CRITICISMS OF POSITIVE LIBERTY

In examining the freedom to do a particular thing in Chapters II and III, I directed a number of criticisms at the negative account of liberty. The dominant theme of my arguments was that there are theoretical difficulties in the negative account which can be eliminated by extending that account in the positive direction. If this move is resisted, the negative account is left with a good deal that is artificial, or at least arbitrary, and in serious need of outside justification – perhaps from deeper reaches of ethical theory or from the requirements of political practice.

Never far from the negative libertarian's mind is the belief that the chief reason for resisting an extension of the account in positive directions is the unacceptability of positive libertarianism once carefully examined. Positive accounts of liberty have been charged with linguistic impropriety, theoretical confusion, violation of deep moral principles, and promotion of totalitarian political practice. If these charges are well founded, then we will, of course, have to make do with a negative account of liberty, whatever its difficulties and whatever the initial attractions of a positive account.

So it is time to see whether a positive account of liberty can be defended against these often aired criticisms. I will not consider all the arguments which have been made against positive liberty. The ones I take up either seem to me to be significant or are representative and have seemed to others to be significant.

20. THAT POSITIVE LIBERTY EXTENDS THE NOTION
TO MEANINGLESSNESS

The following passage, from *The Principles of Political Thought* by S. I. Benn and R. S. Peters, characterizes a view of liberty similar to that developed in Chapters IV and V.

People who approve the spread of state regulation in recent years often try to reconcile it with "liberty" by re-defining that word in terms of opportunity. "Absence of restraint," it is said, is too limited a definition; freedom has a positive as well as a negative aspect. If education is expensive and the parents are poor, it makes a mockery of freedom to say that one is free to educate one's children, merely because there is no law or custom against it. Choice may be *formally* unlimited; there can be no freedom unless it is also *effectively* unlimited. To remove any hindrance to people doing what they want to do thus counts as an extension of freedom. To provide a cripple with an artificial leg, an ignorant man with education, an unemployed man with a job, all count as positive extensions of freedom. Legal compulsions are then a small price to pay for positive freedoms of this sort; for we yield a little only to receive back more. And the absolute goodness of freedom ramains intact.[1]

I quote this at length, first, to show the similarity to the account of Chapters IV and V. For clarity, I should point out, however, that the similarity is not total. For example, there is the suggestion that freedom is only extended when we remove a hindrance to something *wanted*. As discussed earlier, it is an extension, though typically a lesser one, when we remove a hindrance to something unwanted as well. Also, legal compulsions may or may not be a cost worth paying to extend, say, opportunity. It depends on the legal compulsion and on the opportunity. Legal compulsions are restrictions of positive liberty, sometimes very considerable restrictions.

The chief reason, however, that I have quoted the above passage in its entirety is to avoid the suspicion that I have left something out which would make Benn and Peters' criticism more responsive to the positive account they characterize. The following passage comes immediately after the one quoted above.

The trouble with this interpretation of freedom as a political ideal is that it excludes nothing. Any condition can be described as the absence of its opposite. If health is "freedom from disease," and education "freedom from ignorance," there is no conceivable object of social organization and action that cannot be called "freedom." But the price of making "freedom" all-embracing as a social end is to drain it of all descriptive meaning, and to leave only the prescriptive overtones, to make it synonymous with the vaguest terms of approval like "good" and "desirable."[2]

The charge that is here leveled against the positive account is a serious one – that, ultimately, it lacks content. But the argument backing up the charge does not seem entirely appropriate. In fact, I cannot read this passage without wondering whether something was accidentally cut out of the previous passage which made relevant bringing up "freedom from disease." Perhaps in an earlier draft, the liberty-as-opportunity argument was "buttressed" by claims reminiscent of Roosevelt's "Four Freedoms."

I am in agreement with Benn and Peters that the "freedom from" locution has nothing directly to do with liberty either as a personal or social ideal. Automobiles can be (if seldom are) free from defects. Freedom from hunger or disease has as much to do with liberty as does freedom from defects. These are simply ways of expressing the absence of something undesirable. Of course, one will not be able to do as much if one is not free from hunger or disease, but then one may not be able to do as much if one's car is not free from defects. Note that "freedom from decisions" makes perfectly good sense. One can even find it occasionally in travel brochures. But to be free from all decisions would be to have no liberty. "Freedom from liberty" is a little odd, since the positive connotations of "liberty" are so strong. But we have no trouble understanding it, and it is not too hard to construct a context in which some authoritarian (or existentialist) would make serious use of this phrase. What all this shows is that identifying liberty with "freedom from" is at best obviously false. It makes the scope of liberty impossibly broad, and likely leads to straightforward contradiction.

However, positive accounts of liberty in no way depend upon conflating "freedom from" and "freedom." Indeed, the rendition of positive liberty given by Benn and Peters, which is supposed to be the target of criticism, does not make this mistake.

Even if positive liberty does not get into trouble in this particular way, however, it might still be so broad as to lose all content. After all, on the positive conception, liberty is undeniably broader than it is on the negative conception. The conclusion of Benn and Peters might be right even if part of their argument seems to be off on a tangent. Does positive liberty, or "liberty-as-alternatives," become an all-embracing social good? Positive liberty does "include" the artificial leg and enough to eat to have alternatives requiring physical strength.

One might take Benn and Peters to claim that on the positive account, "maximum social liberty" is equivalent in meaning to "greatest social good." But even if this equivalence held, "the greatest social good" has content. ("Greatest social good" is not equivalent to "good." And the view that "good," itself, expresses only vague approval is, at least, controversial.) But this argument is unnecessary. A positive account of liberty does not establish a meaning equivalence between "maximum social liberty" and "greatest social good," since liberty positively conceived is not extensionally equivalent to the whole of the social good. Happiness, the absence of pain, justice, love, beauty, and more, are good things quite distinct from alternatives, options, and opportunities.

Many other good things have *some* relation to positive liberty. For example, one usually cannot do as much if one is in excruciating pain. Still, absence of excruciating pain is not the same thing as the alternatives it opens up. Moreover, some pains do not restrict our alternatives, and liberty is certainly not the only reason we value the absence of pain. The reader can verify that similar relations hold between liberty and other good things. In short, positive liberty, though broader than negative liberty, is not so broad as to become equivalent to "the good" or even "the social good." So the basic idea of the Benn and Peters "lack of content" argument is mistaken.

Joel Feinberg makes a slightly different "no content" criticism of positive accounts of liberty. He notes all the things one may be incapable of doing such as being a weight-lifting champion, or Winston Churchill, walking on the sun, and both existing and not existing at the same time. He then argues as follows:

Although the line between inabilities that are also unfreedoms and those that are not is obviously hard to draw, we should make every effort to draw it with precision, for unless *some* incapacities are *not* considered to be unfreedoms, perfect freedom itself will be an utterly empty and unapproachable ideal.[3]

So unlike Benn and Peters, who claim that positive liberty loses content because we would have to call anything good "liberty," Feinberg takes positive liberty to be an impossible, and hence contentless, social ideal.

Consider an example of a simple impossible ideal: "being a round square." This is certainly an unattainable ideal and, I suppose, even an unapproachable one. (I will resist the temptation to say one might *approach* it by becoming round.) It is also empty in one sense. It has no realizations. But many realizable and important ideals are equally empty in that sense. We realize relatively few of our ideals. So "having no realizations" is not, I take it, Feinberg's sense of "empty." Rather, this word is intended to mean something closer to "meaningless," "content-less," or "non-functional." But so understood, Feinberg is, I believe, in error.

If "round square" were meaningless, we would not be able to demonstrate that there can be no such thing as a round square. To see that an impossible ideal is not contentless, consider the null ideal – the ideal satisfied by every possible state of affairs. This ideal has the very best claim to be without content as an ideal. Its content is not sufficient to rule out anything. Making the natural assumption that ideals with the same content are identical, the hypothesis that an impossible ideal is content-less entails that one and the same ideal has no realizations and that everything is a realization of it.

Moreover, though impossible ideals are unattainable, they may still function as ideals. People do pursue impossible dreams. Witness the long search for a method of "squaring the circle." So an impossible ideal, while unapproachable, is neither meaningless, nor contentless, nor non-functional in the sense of being incapable of guiding conduct.

An ideal which includes both unrealizable and realizable elements is in even better shape. While it is unrealizable as a whole, it may be partially realized. Consider a list of things our indigent dishwasher is personally unfree to do: walking on the sun, both existing and not existing at the same time, . . . vacationing on the Riviera. From this list we can conclude that the dishwasher will never be perfectly free. But that is hardly surprising. It is a thesis of a positive account that personal freedom is never perfect. The goal is not perfect freedom but increased freedom. (Similarly, utilitarianism does not seek perfect happiness, whatever that might be, but the maximization of happiness.) And our dishwasher's freedom can certainly be increased; by making him free to vacation on the Riviera.

In short, where the goal is understood as increased freedom rather than perfect freedom, there is no problem in including impossible alternatives on the list of unfreedoms. They don't make the ideal empty, meaningless, contentless, or non-functional. Impossibilities can be quietly ignored while one works on the possibilities. We can thus save ourselves from what Feinberg grants is a hard exercise in line drawing – separating the mere inabilities from the unfreedoms. (If one must draw a line, the one I use for social liberty, defined in terms of impossibilities on every social arrangement, has a good deal to recommend it.)

I conclude that neither Feinberg nor Benn and Peters have shown that positive liberty extends that notion to meaninglessness, nor to the point that it ceases to function as a social ideal. Nor, I think, is it likely that such an argument can be found. The characterization of positive liberty in Chapters IV and V seems to have no such consequences. Moreover, it would be a little surprising if an approach which has stirred such controversy, and is taken by both friends and enemies to have policy implications, should turn out to be literally devoid of content.

21. LIBERTY AND ITS CONDITIONS OF EXERCISE

I want now to consider two related criticisms that Berlin makes of views similar to the one I am arguing for. Such views are accused of confusing liberty with the conditions of its exercise and of confusing liberty with the conditions which give it value. Though Berlin seems to think of these as being a single confusion, I will separate them.

It is important to discriminate between liberty and the conditions of its exercise. If a man is too poor or too ignorant or too feeble to make use of his legal rights, the liberty that these rights confer upon him is nothing to him, but it is not thereby annihilated.[4]

Berlin is certainly right that we should distinguish between legal liberty and its conditions of exercise. I am legally free to run a four minute mile, but lack the physical constitution required to exercise this liberty. You are legally free to walk away from the kidnappers who hold you at gunpoint, but you cannot exercise this freedom because of the coercion involved. In the terms of MacCallum's triadic analysis, the conditions of the exercise of a liberty are simply all the conditions which must be absent for you to carry out the action, if you choose to do so, *minus* the preventing conditions specified by the species of liberty. Since different species of liberty have different preventing conditions, they also have different conditions of exercise.

Of course, it is possible to include so much in the preventing conditions that the liberty defined would have no additional conditions of exercise. Personal freedom, as I characterize it, has this property. This cannot, however, instructively be put in the simple form that if A is personally free to do x, then A does x if A chooses to do x. This formulation will not do because personal freedom is always a matter of degree, and while that degree may be 0, it does not seem, strictly speaking, that it can be 1. (As previously discussed, however, when the probability that A will succeed in doing x is very close to 1, it will be perfectly reasonable to say 'A is free to do x' as a shorthand for 'A is highly free to do x.') The way to put the all-embracing nature of personal freedom's preventing conditions is that anything, other than A's autonomous choice (and the non-coercive reasons A takes into account) which might result in A's not doing x, tends to lower A's degree of freedom to do x.

So while social liberty has both preventing conditions and other conditions of exercise, personal freedom does not. If anyone is guilty of the confusion Berlin criticizes, then, I should be a prime candidate. But there is no confusion. I have simply drawn the line between the preventing conditions which define liberty and those other conditions which may stand in the way of its exercise in a way different from Berlin's own preferred way. And of course this I have done with social liberty as well as personal freedom, although in the former case the disagreement with Berlin is not quite so great. To avoid taking Berlin's charge of confusion to be nothing more than rhetorical special pleading, it is, I think, best to construe it as the claim that drawing too inclusive a line around the defining preventing conditions destroys the *utility* of a notion of freedom, at least for the purposes of political philosophy. Berlin does have arguments relevant to this more fitting charge. Some of them are apparently of an "ordinary language" sort and similar to those that will be discussed in Section 23. Then there is a policy argument which I will consider in the course of discussing the second half of the confusion Berlin purports to find.

22. LIBERTY AND THE CONDITIONS THAT GIVE IT WORTH

Berlin distinguishes between liberty and the "conditions in which alone its possession is of value."[5] The latter include knowledge, health, and presumably, economic sufficiency. Similarly, John Rawls distinguishes between liberty and the worth of liberty.

The inability to take advantage of one's rights and opportunities as a result of poverty and ignorance, and a lack of means generally, is sometimes counted among the constraints definitive of liberty. I shall not, however, say this, but rather I shall think of these things as affecting the worth of liberty.[6]

Unlike Berlin, Rawls does not call the failure to make this distinction a confusion, but he does think that the distinction is morally important. The principles of justice must treat liberty and the worth of liberty in fundamentally different ways.

If we take seriously the distinction between liberty and what gives liberty value or worth, we are forced to say that liberty is of no value in the absence of these other conditions. From that it would seem to follow that any policy directed towards the attainment of liberty would be irrational if it were not also directed towards the attainment of what makes liberty valuable. So if we call liberty plus what makes liberty valuable "the liberty complex," it would seem to be a rational policy to maximize (or maximize under an equality constraint, or maximize the minimum level of) the liberty complex. And if the liberty complex plays this key role in our policy, while liberty itself does not, and if the liberty complex is, in fact, just like liberty except that it has a somewhat wider set of defining preventing conditions, then why not redeploy our terminology somewhat, renaming the liberty complex "liberty"? That a wider set of preventing conditions makes liberty a value of direct concern to moral and political philosophy is surely, itself, a reason to use that wider definition. We ought to be given good reasons, then, not to use the wider set, but instead to exclude, with Berlin and Rawls, such matters as economic conditions from the defining preventing conditions of liberty.

Both Rawls and Berlin do have reasons, though it seems to me that in neither case are they satisfactory. Norman Daniels in his excellent paper, "Equal Liberty and Unequal Worth of Liberty",[7] examines Rawls' reasons in considerable detail. It seems to me that Daniels is fundamentally right both that the distinction between liberty and the worth of liberty is arbitrary on its own terms and that the distinction will not do the work Rawls asks of it. In particular, it will not do the work Rawls asks of it because it is not, Daniels argues, rational within Rawls' own framework to treat liberty and the worth of liberty in different ways – requiring equal liberty but subjecting the worth of liberty to the "difference principle" (maximizing the minimum level of primary goods). While I am in the main convinced by Daniels' arguments, I wonder about recasting Rawls' account to give a special place to everyone's achieving a certain (in principle specifiable) minimum worth of liberty, which I will call the "threshold."

Suppose that we are unwilling (in the original position) to risk falling below a given threshold worth of a selected set of "basic liberties" while above that point an increase in the worth of these liberties is merely desirable. Suppose as well, that everyone's (equally) having the liberties (defined narrowly) plus the society's not being too poor (to insure that the "special conception" of justice applies),[8] plus the operation of the second principle with respect to "primary goods," guarantees that the threshold worth of the basic liberties will be attained by everyone. We require this much, but beyond this we are willing that any additional worth of liberty be subject to the operation of the second principle on the whole class of primary goods. Understood in this way, the two principles become roughly equivalent to:

(1) First, insure that everyone achieves at least a certain specified threshold level of worth of the basic liberties.
(2) Then, maximize the level of primary goods of a representative member of the worst-off class.

This reconstruction does not seem entirely compatible with everything Rawls says, but it does seem to me to catch something of his intention in treating liberty and the worth of liberty in different ways. So understood, the distinction between liberty and its worth does do some work. For example, if we took liberty more broadly to include those economic preventing conditions which Rawls says give liberty its worth, then we would not necessarily get a result compatible with the one given by the above two principles if we substitute for the first principle either a maximization of basic liberty under quality or a maximization of the minimum level of basic liberty. Either of these courses might cost too much in terms of the minimum level of the whole set of primary goods.

But even if the distinction between liberty and the worth of liberty does do this work, it does not seem to be the clearest or most efficient way of doing it. For one thing, it leaves vague the crucial question of just what the threshold level of the worth of liberty is. We can gather, I think, that actually being able to form your own religious opinions is included, while (to borrow Daniels' example) being able to take an expensive religious pilgrimage would be excluded. The economic and other enabling conditions required to think your own thoughts are relatively easy to come by in a non-subsistence economy (if we are not too demanding about what is to count as *your own*). The wherewithal for a pilgrimage may not be so easy to come by. And it does seem initially plausible that being able to think your own thoughts on religious topics is something we would not want to risk, while we would perhaps be willing to let the pilgrimage compete with other goods under the second principle. But the principle that the "thought side" of the liberty of conscience is more important than its action side needs some serious argument in the light of the fact that some religions themselves do not count the actions required by the faith any less important than the required states of mind. And in the original position we must take into account that it may be such a religion that we embrace on the other side of the veil of ignorance.

To sum up, it may be Rawls' purpose to say that we would not risk in the original position falling below a certain threshold level of worth of the basic liberties, but that this level will automatically be met if we have the liberties "themselves" (legal liberty, non-interference) in the context of moderate scarcity, and the second principle. But if this is his intent, it would be better to spell this out explicitly so that we could examine the specifics of the threshold level of the worth of liberty, the reasons for taking it to have a special status, and the claim that it will automatically be met under the three conditions just mentioned. When all this is successfully worked out, I think Rawls' position, if basically correct, would more helpfully be put in terms of a distinction between privileged and non-privileged liberties rather than between liberty and the worth of liberty. In any event, I do not think that Rawls has yet given us a convincing reason to accept the latter distinction.

Berlin's justification for the distinction between liberty and what gives it value is a little easier to follow than Rawls', but it is, I think, more clearly unsatisfactory. Berlin grants that what has value is the complex consisting of liberty and the absence of such other conditions as poverty and ignorance. But he insists on segregating these conditions into two classes even though that prevents our taking social liberty to be itself valuable and hence a self-sufficient, if incomplete, part of the social ideal. Berlin's explanation is that the word "liberty" has a special protective function that should not be spread too thin. The absence of human restraint, compulsion, and coercion are more in need of protection than are the other conditions in the liberty complex.

In their zeal to create social and economic conditions in which alone freedom is of genuine value, men tend to forget freedom itself; and if it is remembered, it is liable to be pushed aside to make room for these other values with which the reformers and revolutionaries have become preoccupied.[9]

Aside from the repetition of the bald assertion that social freedom does not embrace the social and economic conditions which make it possible for people to exercise their legal freedoms, what we have here is an empirical claim. Those who would change society to realize roughly the sort of thing I have called "positive liberty" will tend to emphasize economic and social reform and lose sight of the importance of legal liberty, in particular, and the absence of constraint, in general. The policy conclusion that follows from this empirical claim is not that the whole ideal should be abandoned, but that the use of "liberty" should be restricted so as to protect that part of the ideal that is likely to be lost sight of.

I'm not sure that the word "liberty" would be strong enough to protect us from restraint and coercion if such a tendency actually exists. I have further doubts that the way political philosophers use the word is of so much significance in practical politics. Political leaders are quite capable of using language in ways unsanctioned by political philosophers. So the policy conclusion is dubious even if the empirical claim is correct. But I find the empirical claim quite dubious itself.

What is Berlin taking as evidence of the political practice of those who take economic conditions as partly constitutive of liberty? If he has in mind the Russian experience, it seems to me he is being entirely too sympathetic to Stalin and his successors. It is not that Stalin lost sight of the importance of the absence of coercion while building up the material conditions of liberty. He drastically cut back liberty on all fronts to insure the dominance and security (especially the military security) of the bureaucratic class which he represented and which still rules Russia. The last vestiges of anything that could be called "positive libertarianism" in the Russian revolutionary movement were liquidated at the onset of the Stalin period. (It is a matter of debate to what extent left libertarianism and associated ultra-democratic views were present in the Bolshevik Party. My own reading is that they were fairly well represented. They were, however, forced into the background by the civil war, without much apology, and never reappeared.)

In fact, political practice guided by a positive libertarian vision is, I think, rare. In the cases I know of where it did arguably appear in a mass movement, it was not corrupted by too great a concern for things economic, but either overwhelmed by quite different political ideals or else simply crushed by outside military force as in the cases of the Paris Commune and Hungarian rebellion against the Soviets. So it appears that the empirical backing for Berlin's claim is lacking.

I do not deny that there are those who speak of liberty and intend, at most, certain "welfarist" components of the ideal. Against such people it is important constantly to emphasize the negative side of liberty. Certainly, if one were in Russia today, and could do so without being whisked off to a mental hospital, one should preach the gospel of the absence of restraint and coercion.

But Berlin is not in Russia. He is a member of a society which glaringly fails to provide for many of its citizens the material support necessary for free activity. Thus arise great discrepancies in what, for Berlin, gives liberty its value. In this context, to reserve "liberty" for the absence of restraint and coercion is a conservative betrayal of the broader ideal to which Berlin claims allegiance. It plays into the hands of those who don't believe that adequate health care or education or a reasonable level of income have anything to do with the value of liberty.

In short, by drawing the lines between preventing conditions and conditions of exercise the way he does, by separating liberty from the "conditions in which alone its possession is of value," Berlin tends to defend the Western *status quo*. Perhaps Berlin believes that *status quo* to be preferable to any system which reformers or revolutionaries would be likely to bring about – whatever their political ideals (even if they share his own). This pessimistic claim would obviously demand a great deal of support, and it would seem that much of the relevant evidence lies in the future.

I speculate that Berlin's separation of liberty from its conditions of value, as well as the two different tendencies within his account ("alterable practices" versus "the absence of bullying") reflects the fact that Berlin is attracted by a social ideal whose consequences, in terms of political practice, are too radical for him. In any event, to fail to make Berlin's distinctions between liberty and the conditions in which its possession is of value does not reflect confusion. It simply reflects a politics different from Berlin's. That political difference is, at least in part, a matter of degree of optimism about the possible outcomes of reform or revolution.

In addition, though there are only hints of this in *Four Essays on Liberty*, there may be a disagreement as to whether human restraint, compulsion, and coercion are more repugnant than other ways doors may be closed. Probably Berlin believes that they are; certainly most negative libertarians do. To what extent this view is justified will be the topic of the last two sections of this chapter. Before turning to this substantive moral issue, I want to take up one final charge that positive libertarianism has made a fundamental "conceptual" mistake. This is the charge that positive libertarianism misuses language.

23. "LIBERTY" IN ORDINARY LANGUAGE

The belief that positive accounts of liberty are guilty of linguistic improprieties is fairly widespread among Anglo-American philosophers. The charges of confusion and vacuous definition already considered are, of course, matters of linguistic impropriety, broadly speaking. What I want to consider now are somewhat more modest allegations that positive accounts are unfaithful to the ways in which we ordinarily employ the words "freedom" and "liberty." I should add that some philosophers making such charges believe them to be very serious indeed. Probably there are still some who believe that such infidelity to ordinary language is a decisive philosophical objection. This metaphilosophical view, associated with Oxford and once widely popular in Britain and North America, is now, fortunately, fading. More typical is the belief that infidelity to ordinary language is an intellectual sin of modest to moderate proportions, to be avoided where conveniently possible.

Philosophers often seem to rely upon suppressed ordinary language arguments. It is simply announced as a conclusion or a step in an argument that A's could not be B. No theoretical or empirical argument is hinted at that would explain why A's could not be B, but the reader is expected to notice that it would sound very odd to say 'this A is B.' Granted it is sometimes a little hard to tell suppressed ordinary language arguments from simple assumed agreement. (Whatever A's may be, surely we all know they couldn't be B.) But in many cases, unsupported steps are made where prior agreement could not be assumed, and in a large number it is ordinary language that is just off stage. It seems to me that this is an especially common phenomenon in political philosophy, and that critics of positive liberty have used their share of such suppressed arguments.

Obviously, however, ordinary language arguments that are at least partly explicit are easier to deal with. As an example, consider the following argument from P. H. Partridge's article on freedom in the *Encyclopedia of Philosophy*.

It can be said that, at least in many cases, equating freedom with possession of power will involve a distortion of ordinary language. If I ask, "Am I free to walk into the Pentagon?" the question will be clearly understood; but if I ask, "Am I free to walk across the Atlantic Ocean?" the appropriate answer will be, "You are free to, if you can." This suggests the main argument; the linking of "being free to" with "having the capacity or power" deprives the word "free" of its essential and unequivocal function, which is to refer to a situation or state of affairs in which a man's choice of how he acts is not deliberately forced or restrained by another man . . . It may be true to say that the poor man is as free to spend his holidays in Monte Carlo as the rich man is, and true also to say that he cannot afford to do so. These two statements, it is argued, refer to two distinct states of affairs, and nothing is gained by amalgamating them.[10]

Due to the "it is argued," I am not sure whether Partridge wants to associate himself fully with this argument, but that need not concern us. It is reasonably representative of considerations many people have had in mind. So I don't think it will be unfair to take a close look at this argument.

There are three pieces of purported linguistic data used in the argument. The first is that fluent speakers understand the question 'Am I free to walk into the Pentagon?' The second is that 'Am I free to walk across the Atlantic Ocean?' is properly answered by 'You are free to, if you can.' The third is that it may sensibly and truly be said that someone is free to vacation in Monte Carlo although too poor to do so. Let me take up each of these in turn.

It is certainly not deviant or odd to ask the Pentagon question. Whether it will be clearly understood, or not, is another matter. If someone asked me this question while standing near the Pentagon, I might at least wonder whether the question was about the legality of a private citizen's entering the Pentagon or about the presence or absence of a guard who would turn one back. If I were a tour guide, the question might even be seeking my permission to enter the Pentagon. The possible ambiguities in this case result from the fact that there are different species of freedom which might be intended. Sometimes such ambiguity is benign. The Pentagon, for example, might be neither guarded nor illegal to enter, and I might be willing to grant my permission. So I could simply say 'Yes.' All this is not to dispute Partridge's main point. The question is perfectly sensible in English. But it is worth bearing in mind that it is not entirely unambiguous between different species of freedom.

A very different matter is the question, 'Am I free to walk across the Atlantic Ocean?' While not deviant grammatically or semantically, it is certainly difficult to interpret in any clear and sensible way. This is because there is no species of freedom that the questioner can reasonably be taken as inquiring after, if he or she has anything approaching average rationality and knowledge. It cannot be legal freedom that is in question, because everyone knows legislators rarely prohibit what is physically impossible. For the same sort of reason, it cannot be positive liberty because the questioner must know, if rational, that he or she lacks the capacity to walk across the ocean. Other species of liberty are either inapplicable or give equally obvious answers, either negative or affirmative. So, if we think our questioner sincere, I would suppose that the best, and most "ordinary" response would be, 'What do you mean?'

This is to grant, probably even to strengthen, what seems to be part of Partridge's point; the ocean walk question is not a clear, sensible question under most circumstances. But this does not cut against including capacities within the definition of freedom, as Partridge seems to think. It is no more sensible to ask this question about positive freedom than it is about legal freedom. (If anything, there is more point in asking whether it is illegal to do the impossible than whether one is capable of doing it. Doubtless there are laws against certain impossible actions.) A positive account of freedom in no way encourages or licenses this sort of question, and is no more responsible for its oddity than is any other account of freedom.

The answer that Partridge suggests is proper to the ocean walk question is 'You are free to, if you can.' While this seems to me a distant second best to inquiring after the intent of the question, it is not itself deviant. It is also not crystal clear. My guess is that Partridge intends it to be roughly equivalent to the following philosophically partisan reply. 'It is not against the law, and no one will stop you; so you are *free* to walk across the ocean, though of course you cannot.' I surmise that Partridge understands the reply along these lines because he thinks, wrongly, that the ocean walk question is one which arises from a positive perspective. I will grant that if philosophically untutored speakers would give this expanded version of Partridge's answer, that would provide grist for the negative mill. It would show that the language recognizes negative species of liberty – something I do not at all doubt. It might also tend to show that the speakers give these negative species a certain priority over species of liberty involving capacities. This, however, could be argued, even if untutored speakers were to give the expanded reply. Since Partridge does not explicitly claim that they would give that reply, or that the shorter reply is to be understood in that fashion, I will not pursue that argument further.

It is significant that 'You are free to, if you can,' taken at face value, is a true and sensible response to the ocean walk question on a positive account of personal freedom. The other preventing conditions of personal freedom are absent. Therefore, if you have the physical capacity to walk across the ocean, you are free to do so. On the other hand, the reply which should do the trick for straightforward negative accounts of liberty is simply, 'Yes,' or 'Of course,' since there are no laws or restraints against walking across the ocean. But these answers are very non-ordinary ways of responding to our ocean walk questioner; at least in most circumstances. I shall return to this point shortly.

So even if Partridge were right about the first two items of linguistic data, that would not tend to show that ordinary language does not recognize species of liberty which include incapacities among their preventing conditions. If anything, it is the negative account which has some explaining to do.

Partridge has a second argument which is in somewhat better shape. This argument depends on the linguistic datum that it may be true to say that a person is free to vacation at Monte Carlo and also true to say that the person cannot afford to do so. I grant the evidence. There is a use of "free" on which these statements can be simultaneously true. This is because legal freedom, for example, is a perfectly good species of freedom, and we are legally free to do much that we are unfree to do in other ways. What the linguistic evidence shows is that ordinary language recognizes either legal freedom or, at least, some form of freedom for which impecuniousness is not one of the preventing conditions. However, the argument does not at all establish that ordinary language prohibits, or even lacks, uses of "free" on which impecuniousness is among the preventing conditions.

Consider the following analogous argument. It is true to say of *A* that she is a basketball player. (She plays every chance she gets.) Yet it is false to say that *A* is on the basketball team. Therefore there is no ordinary use of 'basketball player' which requires that the person be a member of the team. The two statements refer to two distinct states of affairs, and nothing is gained by amalgamating them.

The argument is, of course, ludicrous, as is shown by the fact that there is a use of 'basketball player,' familiar to anyone who has gone to school in the United States, which is restricted in its application to members of the school team – usually the men's team, frequently the varsity.

All natural languages are filled with words with multiple uses. For this reason, where the question of linguistic distortion is involved, an argument of the form of Partridge's Monte Carlo argument is entirely inappropriate.

Let me add a comment on Partridge's point about referring to distinct states of affairs. It is surely not the case that wherever there are two ordinary expressions, *F* and *G*, such that *F* refers to *x* and *G* refers to *y*, *x* distinct from *y*, there is no ordinary expression referring to *x* "amalgamated with" *y*. Since the sort of "amalgamation" involved in adding impecuniousness to the preventing conditions of negative liberty is conjunctive, consider another such amalgamation in ordinary language. Let *F* be "warm" and *G* be "humid." These certainly refer to distinct things, yet "muggy," which refers (at least roughly) to their conjunction is itself perfectly good ordinary language.

Of course, we get the possibility of confusion if the expression for the amalgamated state of affairs is the same as one of the original expressions, as in the case of "free." This is a reason for disallowing such expressions in a regimented language, but it is obviously a fact of life of ordinary languages. For the moment, questions of good language policy are not at issue. At issue is only the charge of the distortion of ordinary language.

Let me now examine what I think is the best way to try to discredit the ordinary language credentials of positive liberty. Take cases of incapacity by virtue of physical impossibility. These will give rise to "unfreedoms" on some positive accounts. Yet sentences asserting such unfreedom may strike the ordinary speaker as deviant or obviously false. Consider Helvetius' example (part of which I have already made frequent use of).

The free man is the man who is not in irons, nor imprisoned in a jail, nor terrorized like a slave by the fear of punishment . . . it is not lack of freedom not to fly like an eagle or swim like a whale.[11]

Let us continue to suppose that people are not capable of flying (just) like eagles, and that no social expenditure or arrangement would give anyone this capacity. 'I am unfree to fly like an eagle,' is not, then, true in the sense of social liberty characterized in Chapter V. So far I agree with the negative account. However, the simple negative account takes this sentence to be false. It will be recalled that I take it to be neither true nor false where social liberty is in question.[12]

When it is a matter of positive personal freedom, as characterized in Chapter IV, the test sentence comes out true. Therein lies a major conflict with the negative account. Does positive personal freedom clash, here, with ordinary language? There are certainly conversational contexts in which it would be perfectly natural to say that one is unfree to fly like an eagle. But if someone dropped this comment unprepared into conversation, it would be slightly odd. We would probably ask what the person meant. So some oddness I admit. But oddness by itself does not show too much. It is odd for someone to exclaim on a hot August day, with apparent intent to communicate, "It is not below freezing." The positive libertarian can interpret the oddness of Helvetius' case the same way. 'I am unfree to fly like an eagle' is odd because 'I am incapable of flying like an eagle' is odd.

If the only uses of "free" in ordinary language are simple negative uses, then it should strike ordinary speakers that 'I am unfree to fly like an eagle' is obviously false. That is, it should be received in the same spirit as 'I am over 100 feet tall.' It should be obviously true that I am free to fly like an eagle, since no one prevents me from so doing.

I find it highly unlikely that ordinary speakers would respond to 'I am free to fly just like an eagle' with 'Of course!' More likely seems, 'You're crazy!' or 'What do you mean?' In fact, if either 'I am unfree to fly like an eagle' or 'I am free to fly like an eagle' would strike the ordinary speaker as obviously false, my bet would be on the latter. If I am right, an exclusively negative account of freedom is in worse shape with ordinary language than is an account which embraces positive liberty.

The best tactic for the negative libertarian when it comes to ordinary language is probably to accept truth value gaps in the way I did in Chapter V for social liberty. When something is physically impossible for anyone to do, we say neither that I am free to do it nor that I am unfree to do it. Freedom and unfreedom occur only in those cases where the presence or absence of human interference makes a potential difference. This is not so for physically impossible actions, so in such cases there can be no talk of freedom.

This move neutralizes the objection to the negative account that 'I am free to fly like an eagle' does not strike most ordinary speakers as obviously true. Truth value gaps are also suggested by the fact that 'I am not free to fly like an eagle' seems to be in better ordinary language shape than is 'I am unfree to fly like an eagle.' This may be because the former can be interpreted as 'It is not true to say that I am free to fly like an eagle.'[13]

Let me recapitulate the consequences of different responses to 'I am free to fly like an eagle.' If uncorrupted speakers regard this as obviously true, then simple negative accounts of liberty would be supported. If speakers regard it as neither true nor false, then truth value gap accounts (negative or positive) would be supported. If speakers regard it as false, then ordinary language has a use of freedom corresponding, at least roughly, to the positive personal freedom of Chapter IV. My suspicion is that ordinary speakers would split between the second and third possibilities. Obviously, such a result would do nothing to disconfirm the existence in ordinary language of positive uses of "freedom" like those of Chapters IV and V.

How well do these conclusions from conjectured results hold up against other sorts of cases? If ordinary language has no positive uses of "freedom," that should have a wide range of consequences. 'Having gambled away all his inheritance, he was no longer free to wander from one spa to another' should either seem obviously false or at least strike us as using "free" in a strained or metaphorical sense. I doubt that it does. 'One who is rich and healthy is no freer than one who is poor and ill' should seem clearly and unambiguously true. Would ordinary speakers agree? 'She was free to compete in the marathon with her broken leg, but found herself incapable of doing so' should not sound like a weak pedantic joke.

In short, I think that there is good reason to believe that a scientific sample of the way English is actually spoken would reveal that there are ordinary uses corresponding to the sorts of liberty outlined in Chapters IV and V. (The contrary view may arise from placing too much faith in the linguistic intuitions of those who share a common background and similar political philosophies.) Let me re-emphasize that I am not at all denying that there are ordinary uses corresponding to negative species of freedom. We often talk about legal freedom, for example, without explicitly saying "legal." All I claim is that such uses do not exhaust the ordinary language of freedom and liberty.

I also want to reiterate the position stated in the Introduction: ordinary language is not very important. I would be prepared to break with ordinary language were that necessary. As it happens, it is unnecessary. However, the key questions are not those of usage but of political and moral theory. Ordinary language has frequently been formed by unacceptable theory.

"Liberty" plays a number of roles in British-American political philosophy. To get a political philosophy which is morally sounder, on my view, it is necessary systematically to substitute the notion of positive liberty for that of negative liberty in a wide range of roles. The real issue, then, is what "liberty" ought to refer to in political philosophy. If the answer corresponds to the positive account, we may need to issue warnings that what "liberty" ought to refer to is not what political philosophers have sometimes taken it to refer to. If, contrary to fact, ordinary speakers never used positive notions of freedom, that would simply have to be added as another such warning.

It is always unfortunate, to some degree, to use words differently from the way others do. And I am proposing a use that differs from the chief use of many political philosophers, and perhaps of some ordinary speakers. That leads to the possibility of confusion. But the possibility of confusion about "freedom" and "liberty" can hardly be laid at the feet of the positive account. These words have been highly ambiguous for a very long time. To risk a little additional confusion by altering the defining preventing conditions of accepted political philosophy is a risk worth taking if it leads to an improvement of that theory.

In conclusion, contrary to well known claims, positive accounts of liberty do not involve any significant distortion of ordinary language. They do depart from the usage of the main tradition of British-American political philosophy. That departure is to be justified, ultimately, on substantive moral grounds. It is to the moral questions that I now want to return.

24. THE SPECIAL EVILS OF RESTRAINT AND COERCION

In including physical incapacities, poverty, ignorance, and the like, among the preventing conditions of personal freedom and, where correctable, among the preventing conditions of social liberty as well, I am, of course, stressing the moral similarities of these conditions and the traditional preventing conditions of restraint, compulsion, and coercion. The most telling way to criticize my view, I think, is not to talk about "confusions" or "distortions of language," but rather to show that the moral dissimilarities between, for example, poverty and physical restraint are so great that it would defeat the purposes of moral theory or political philosophy to include them under the same category.

Since the most heated exceptions have been taken to positive accounts in political philosophy, it is the positive social liberty of Chapter V that I will subject to criticisms of the "moral dissimilarity" sort. For concreteness I will examine the claim that failing to enable someone to run (by corrective surgery and physical therapy) is morally very different from (and morally less reprehensible than) coercively preventing someone from running.

One striking difference between coercion and failure to correct a medical condition is that the former is always intentional. (Ignore subtle forms of interpersonal manipulation which might arguably be called "unconscious coercion".) The coercer intends a restriction of your alternatives. On the other hand, someone who could, but does not, open up added alternatives for you need not intend or desire that your alternatives be no wider than they are. This suggests that evil intent might be what makes coercion worse than failing to enable. This cannot be right, however. Not only are some failings to enable done with the very worst motives, but some of the most intolerable forms of coercion flow from the best of motives. Defenders of liberty have rightly refused to condemn coercion any less because it was intended to be beneficial.

A more plausible suggestion is that eliminating most cases of private coercion is a feasible project. It does not make impossible demands upon people. On the other hand, eliminating a large percentage of the eliminable incapacities of people would be impossibly demanding. Certainly it is a very rigorous morality that demands individual charity wherever the potential benefactor has more alternatives than the potential beneficiary.

The problem here is, of course, one of degree and number. Suppose that there were only one person in need of corrective surgery (or similar help) and that I am the only one who could finance it. Suppose further that doing so would represent no very considerable drain on my resources. In this case, if I am sware of the need, I would be under an obligation to help. Such an obligation no longer represents an unreasonably demanding morality, and the moral differences between refusing to provide corrective surgery and coercively preventing someone from running diminish considerably. My refusal to help would prevent the person from running.

We have quite a different situation, again, with respect to the rigorousness of the morality, when we shift our attention from the obligations of individuals to the obligations of society as a whole, represented by government. Unlike the individual, it will be relatively easy for a government to locate the cases of eliminable serious incapacities. The government will frequently also be in a position to know that if it does not supply the aid, the incapacities will not be eliminated. But the big difference between an individual and the government is, of course, resources. Even the collective resources of the society may be insufficient to eliminate all significant eliminable incapacities. On the other hand, a class of disabilities, defined in terms both of their seriousness and the ease of their correctability, might well be the subject of a governmental program which would put no serious drain on the society's resources. In particular, this use of resources might diminish insignificantly the alternatives of the rest of society; the tax burden for this purpose being, relatively, so small.

This is enough to convince me that there are crippled persons for whom our unwillingness to finance corrective surgery and physical therapy, through the government, is not morally permissible. It is no more permissible than it would be to pass a law prohibiting certain classes of persons from going faster than a walking pace while on foot. So the rigorousness of the associated morality is not a good general reason to take coercion to be an especially unacceptable way of limiting alternatives. At least some failures to enable are, in this respect, in the same moral boat.[14]

Another possibility is that restraint, compulsion, and coercion are morally worse than not enabling because they represent the imposition of one person's will upon another person. Even when the imposed will is well meaning, we may rightly resent its imposition.

But failing to enable someone to do something is sometimes a matter of my imposing my will upon that person. Suppose I refuse to aid someone with the intention of keeping his or her alternatives circumscribed. Forbearing in such a case is just as much an instrument of will as acting.

Still, most cases of failing to enable are not like this. Typically, they do not represent an imposition of the will. In these typical cases, is failing to enable less morally serious, for this reason, than restraining, compelling, or coercing? One does, perhaps, feel worse when one's will collides with that of another person than when it collides with non-human obstacles (even if those obstacles could have been removed by someone). We are more likely to feel belittled by coming out second best in a direct clash of wills. Whether inevitable or not, this psychological fact about our reactions might make typical cases of restraint, compulsion and coercion worse, to some degree, than all but the most blatant of failures to enable. But, if so, this difference of degree, turning on psychological reactions, certainly cannot account for the difference in kind negative libertarians seem to see between restraining, compelling and coercing, on the one hand, and failing to enable, on the other. The final and most plausible place to look for that difference in kind is in the structure of human rights.

25. HUMAN RIGHTS, COERCION, AND NON-AID

It is widely thought that typical cases of coercion violate human rights. It is at least less widely thought that typical cases of non-aid violate human rights. So the question of human rights needs to be looked into to resolve the issue whether refusing to aid in the elimination of incapacities is or is not morally similar to coercion.

Those who believe that coercion does, but non-aid does not, violate rights are almost bound to believe, as well, that no one should be forced to aid anyone else. Such people will hold that a positive libertarian social policy violates rights since this policy would, very likely, tax some people against their will, in order that others have a wider effective freedom. So the question of rights is central both to the basic theory of positive liberty and to the political practice toward which it points.

Human rights are frequently talked about very loosely – a tendency which leads to a good deal of confusion and uncertainty as to what is being claimed. To try to avoid such problems, I offer the following definitions in clarification of what I intend by "human rights" in this essay.

D1. *A* has a right to do *x* with respect to a person *B* if and only if *A* is morally permitted to do *x* and *B* is not morally permitted to prevent *A*'s doing *x*.

D2. *A* has a *prima facie* right to do *x* with respect to a person *B* if and only if *A* is morally permitted to do *x* in the absence of good independent moral considerations to the contrary, and *B* is not morally permitted to prevent *A*'s doing *x* without good independent moral reasons for so doing.

D3. *A* has an absolute right to do *x* with respect to *B* if and only if *A* would be morally permitted to do *x* even if there were good independent moral reasons to the contrary, and *B* would not be morally permitted to prevent *A*'s doing *x* even if *B* had good independent moral reasons for so doing.

There are rights to things other than things one does, of course, but the definitions can be amended in obvious, if tedious, ways to cover these other sorts of rights. I will take a right to be a human right only if it meets the following conditions.

C1. Being a human being is a morally sufficient condition of having the right. (It is a moral truth that all human beings have the right.)

C2. It is a right with respect to all persons (claimable against all persons).[15]

As I understand human rights, they need not be self evident. Nor need they be based upon eternal moral law or deep metaphysical properties of human beings; though they might be. They exist if there are the appropriate sorts of obligations and permissions. Roughly, there are human rights if we ought to act as if there were human rights.

The details of these definitions will not play a very large role in what follows except for the basic definition of rights in terms of permissibility and its absence (obligation). Insofar as rights are definable in these terms,

I argue that coercion and refusing to enable do not stand in any fundamentally different relation to rights. If rights are to be distinguished by something outside the constellation of permissions and obligations they give rise to, then it is possible that some of my arguments will misfire. But while the language of rights may have some special complexities, and while rights may or may not *entail* obligations, it does not seem plausible that the moral force of rights could amount to anything other than obligations and permissions.

As a first piece of evidence that there are rights to aid, consider, again, Nozick's drowning swimmer case.[16] Why is it typically coercion if one refuses to take the drowning swimmer aboard unless the swimmer agrees to pay $10,000? The most natural answer is that one usually has an obligation to come to the aid of people in mortal danger, when one can do so without making a serious sacrifice. To threaten to let the swimmer drown is to threaten not to fulfill that obligation. It is a coercive threat just because in the morally expected course of events, one aids a drowning swimmer. So the swimmer has a right to aid (at least *prima facie*).

If the swimmer does not have a right to aid, it becomes quite mysterious why the boater's "offer" counts as a coercive threat. It cannot be simply that the swimmer has "no real choice," since that will be true also in the case of sufficiently attractive offers which are not, intuitively, coercive. What would justify the principle that one is under no obligation to help a drowning swimmer, but if one does go to the rescue, one must not bargain with the swimmer about terms for the rescue? (It is worth noting the obvious fact that we do not prefer the willful non-rescuer to the coercive rescuer.)

It appears, then, that there is sometimes a right to aid. In this case, it can be construed as a conditional human right. It is a human right, even though not all human beings are drowning swimmers and not all persons are in a position to aid. The right which everyone possesses, just by virtue of being a human being, is the right to rescue *if* one is drowning and *if* there are people who can aid without serious sacrifice. Requirement C1 is satisfied because anyone in the same situation has the right to aid. Requirement C2 is satisfied because anyone in the position to aid is required to do so (an obligation which, of course, is cancelled if someone else goes to the rescue with a high probability of success). Perhaps this still does not state the right quite correctly, however. It might be, for example, that Hitler, in the midst of his career, would have had no right to be rescued.[17] This can be taken care of by adding to the antecedent of the conditional right an exception for persons meeting certain descriptions.

Conditional rights have been recognized throughout the human rights tradition. (The right to life, for example, was believed by its early proponents to be compatible with capital punishment.) What sorts of ultimate moral bases for human rights are compatible with what sorts of conditional rights is an interesting question which I will not pursue here.

Given that there is intuitive evidence of some rights to aid, are there any theoretical considerations to back up this evidence? Perhaps this is one of those points at which our intuitions have been corrupted. In the extreme case of life saving aid, it is obvious that we are perilously close to inconsistency if we prohibit murder but take as morally permitted non-aid when the aid necessary to save life could be given easily. More generally, wherever aid makes a great difference to the beneficiary at small cost to the benefactor, the right to such aid is something it is rational to want in a moral system. It is a highly desirable form of "social insurance" to have it as the accepted practice that boaters pull drowning swimmers from the water. On a wide range of subjective and ideal contract theories of morality, this fact will already be enough to constitute the existence of a right to aid (perhaps *prima facie*). On other theories, the rationality of the practice of aid should, at least, provide a presumption that there is such a right.

Aid of the sort in question is also suggested by the requirement that morality take one person's interests as seriously as another's. Consider a morality which permits A not to come to B's aid in a life and death situation simply because it is slightly inconvenient for A to do so. It may look as if such a morality counts A's convenience more important than B's life.

B might well wonder, in such a situation, whether the morality was in any position to ask for his or her loyalty. In general, it is dubious that a moral system which recognizes no right to aid could command our respect and allegiance. If not, it will fail to guide conduct, and so cease to function as a moral system. This may not count against the truth of the morality on some super-objective meta-ethical theories, but for most such theories moral intuition has to play a large role. The unintuitiveness of the non-aid feature then becomes decisive by itself.

In short, there are general considerations looking to moral theory which support the existence of a right to aid. To reinforce this conclusion, it will be useful to look a little deeper into the foundations of rights. I take it that part of the support for human rights comes from the conviction that each of us has a special relation to his or her own body (at least while alive) and to his or her own states of consciousness. My body, my thought, and my sensations are "mine" in a sense stronger than that of mere ownership. For this reason, I am free to cause myself to be in pain in a wide range of circumstances where others do not have this liberty. I can make decisions about my body and its activity which it is no one else's place to make.

I will say that such matters fall within one's "personal sphere." At least one function which philosophers have had in mind for human rights is that protection of the personal sphere. This gives human rights much of their special character. The boundaries of the personal sphere will not, however, be the same as those of the "morally protected sphere." I am not morally allowed to do just anything I might want to do with my body; like taking it to the showroom and driving off in the car of my choice without paying. Nor are my states of consciousness protected against all unpleasantness – for example, that attendant upon losing a competition.

It is obvious that some refusals to enable fall within the protected sphere of the agent. The poor person may properly refuse to contribute to a scholarship fund benefiting those of middle income. It is equally obvious that some cases of coercion infringe the protected sphere of their target and do not fall within the protected sphere of the coercer. Does refusal to aid ever fall outside the protected sphere of the refuser and infringe the protected sphere of the person refused? We could examine this question by using the drowning swimmer example again. This is not only a refusal to aid, but a refusal to aid of the sort that runs counter to positive liberty, since death is an incapacitation. But let me consider instead a case which involves a more central example of enabling aid. We have not yet seen any specific theoretical justification for a right to such aid.

Suppose that Oscar's blindness could be cured by an operation which Paula, the only available surgeon, chooses not to perform. She so chooses because the operation would take two hours which she would rather spend playing polo. Is Paula morally obligated to perform the operation despite her preferences?

One's seeing is normally something that is within the personal sphere. In large part, it is also within the protected sphere. One ought to be able to see what one wants, so long as it is not the legitimate secret or private preserve of some other person or organization. A very considerable control over visual states of consciousness ought to be vested in the person whose consciousness it is. The blind person lacks this control. Is it wrong to withhold it, when it would be easy to supply it? I think that it is. It might be argued, however, that taking away control over something in the personal sphere (as coercion does) and refusing to bring such control about are two very different things. The personal sphere is protected from such takings away but is not protected against failures to give. This seems to me a little like saying that I may not steal your wolfhound, but am under no obligation to return it if it jumps the fence into my yard.

To examine this question further, suppose that, as the result of something going spectacularly wrong in the alchemical experiments of a distant forbear, one member of your family in each generation falls under "the curse of the ring." The ring in question has the property that whoever wears it, unless it be the cursed person, feels no pain. Any pain the wearer would feel is miraculously transferred to and felt full force by the cursed one, who currently, unluckily, is you.

Quincy, the ring's owner and wearer, argues that he is under no obligation either to give you the ring or to destroy it. He came into possession of the ring quite legally, through a series of voluntary transfers. Of course, while wearing the ring, he has a partial control over your states of consciousness, but he has not taken this control from you. Given the curse, you never had it. He contends, then, that the control over your consciousness which he has lies within his protected sphere. For you to alienate it by taking the ring against his will, would violate his rights.

It seems clear to me that Quincy is wrong about this, but it is not entirely easy to say why. Your pain is within your personal sphere, and *prima facie* you ought to have more control of it than someone else. But the same thing can be said for Quincy, who would lose a great deal of control over his pain if he gave up the ring. Intuitively, the unfairness of Quincy's foisting his pain off on you makes it a more serious intrusion into your personal sphere than the intrusion into Quincy's personal sphere of a moral requirement that he give up this special sort of control over his own pain. What is clearest in this case is that Quincy's possession of such large scale control over your pain is objectionable, even if he did not take it from you in any strong sense of "take."

Now suppose Roger had a ring which, so long as it exists, renders you incapable of seeing. The ring is of modest monetary and some sentimental value to Roger, and he refuses to have it destroyed. This refusal is, if anything, more objectionable than Quincy's, since Quincy's interest in his ring was greater. Clearly, you have a right to the destruction of Roger's ring (perhaps compensating him).

But surely Roger's situation is not significantly different from that of our surgeon, Paula. Instead of a ring of modest value, Paula must give up two hours of time to cure Oscar's blindness. The decision how Paula is to use her time and deploy her surgical talents is normally her own business. It ceases to be, however, if she has the time available, someone has a surgical need this pressing, and if there are not too many such cases. Oscar's need under these circumstances creates a moral claim which Paula cannot deflect. He has a right to her enabling aid, and she has no right to withhold it. I conclude that considerations of autonomy over one's personal sphere reveal no fundamental moral difference between suitably similar cases of coercing and refusing to enable. Where we are sometimes misled, on this point, is by inessential features statistically more frequently found in one kind of case than in the other.

Let me now move on to the question whether it is ever legitimate to force someone to give aid. Even if *A* is morally obligated to do *x*, it might be a violation of A's rights to force A to do x. One way to deal with this issue is in terms of the seriousness of A's obligation to do x and the seriousness of the means which would be required to force A to fulfill that obligation. This will likely lead to an analysis in terms of *prima facie* rights, which would establish the permissibility of enforcing obligations to aid in at least some cases.

Obviously, this would all be congenial to my purposes. Instead of pursuing things in this way, however, I want to take a look at the position that we may never force people to aid others because that is a form of involuntary sacrifice. Absolute rights, some believe, protect against involuntary sacrifice. This seems to be Nozick's position in *Anarchy, State, and Utopia*, and it is Nozick's account and arguments that I will examine. I should hasten to add that I do not assume that Nozick would agree with the conclusions I have already reached as to the existence of rights to enabling aid. I am not sure that Nozick now believes that there is ever a right to aid, though he may have believed that when he wrote "Coercion." It should, perhaps, be possible to make a limited right of this sort compatible with *Anarchy, State, and Utopia*. In any event, some of Nozick's arguments against involuntary sacrifice are presumably intended to cut against any very robust right to aid as well.

On Nozick's theory, rights operate as independent "side constraints" upon actions. This means that the moral structure is not designed to minimize the weighted total of violations of rights, but instead forbids outright actions which violate rights. I may not violate even one right of one person in order to prevent *others* from violating the rights of many.[18] A moral action may not violate rights period. We are not told what to do if we are placed in a situation where any action we might perform, including inaction, violates rights. It is also left unclear how we are to determine whether an action itself violates rights, or merely has consequences that eventuate in the violation of rights. But the basic idea of Nozick's moral theory is clear enough. It is, to put it a little unsympathetically, a "clean hands" morality. The amount of evil in the world is (at most) a secondary matter. What is crucial is that the agent perform no impure act.

Rights understood in this way will, of course, tend to forbid involuntary sacrifices. This is, in fact, one of Nozick's central moral claims. It is grounded on "the underlying Kantian principle that individuals are ends and not merely means; they may not be sacrificed ... without their consent."[19] (It is worth noting, in passing, that this way of stating the Kantian principle does not rule out paternalistic coercion.)[20] In arguing for this principle, Nozick emphasizes the distinctness of persons.

... there is no *social entity* with a good that undergoes some sacrifice for its own good. There are only individual people, different individual people, with their own individual lives. Using one of these people for the benefit of others, uses him and benefits the others. Nothing more . . . To use a person in this way does not sufficiently respect and take account of the fact that he is a separate person, that his is the only life he has. *He* does not get some overbalancing good from his sacrifice, and no one is entitled to force this upon him.[21]

The distinctness of moral subjects is certainly a necessary condition for moral prohibitions on involuntary sacrifice. Imagine an intelligent species that shares a single consciousness through instantaneous and complete telepathy. An injury to one is literally an injury to all. Such creatures would presumably have little understanding of involuntary sacrifice and no use for a prohibition against it.[22]

However, in the case of human beings, the distinctness of persons provides no affirmative argument for Nozick's position but only rebuts a weak and wrong-headed argument in favor of the permissibility of involuntary sacrifice. If the only reason for aggregating and comparing the goods of different persons were the belief that some group mind or other social entity *has* the social good, in the way that we each have our own good, then the practice would, surely, be a misguided one. The real reason for aggregating and comparing goods, of course, is that morality is social in the straightforward sense that different persons are joint participants in it. As a joint participant, one person's pleasures, pains, likes, dislikes, plans, and purposes are at least potentially morally relevant to other persons. This being the case, "organicist" premises are not required to justify some involuntary sacrifice.

Particularly plausible are small involuntary sacrifices which prevent much greater losses by others. We feel no compunction in moving a woman in labor to the front of the line at a taxi stand, even over the objections of some of those in line, unless their need for the taxi is as pressing as hers. Similarly, if an immunity in my blood (and only mine) can save many lives, I may be required, I would think, to give a pint of blood against my will.

It might be thought that Nozick could deny that the taxi case, or even the blood case, is a counterexample to his position. Perhaps one does not have a right to one's place in the taxi line (or one's blood?) when a medical emergency develops. Therefore, one has nothing to sacrifice. But this re-definition of "sacrifice" would be pretty *ad hoc*. Worse from Nozick's perspective, it would threaten to let everything I would call "involuntary sacrifice" in by the back door, with no principle for drawing the line. So I think we can assume that Nozick would not pursue this suggestion.

I would argue that to fail to enforce such involuntary sacrifices as occur in the taxi and pint of blood cases would be to give one person's interests or choices too much weight as against the needs of others. Again, this "weighing" does not at all depend on the existence of a composite subject, but simply on the recognition that each of the distinct participants has a stake in the moral system.

Major involuntary sacrifices raise at least one additional issue not present in the case of minor involuntary sacrifices. Both strenuous obligations and enforcement of strenuous obligations on unwilling agents risk straining the allegiance of people to the moral system. This general problem was already discussed in the previous section. It might put some limits on positive libertarian social policy – say, in its redistributions. It would not prevent such a policy altogether. A larger tax bite is only rarely an extreme sacrifice.

So this investigation of rights has neither turned up any morally important difference between coercing and refusing to enable, nor has it found any basis for the claim that it always violates rights to force one person to aid another. I do not doubt that people will assert that the "real" structure of rights does forbid all involuntary aid or does protect against coercion but not against refusing to enable. Assertion without argument is very popular when it comes to rights. All I can reply is that I see no reason to believe these assertions, and the various arguments given above provide some reason to disbelieve them.

CHAPTER VII

THE VALUE OF LIBERTY

If one thinks of liberty not as the absence of certain sorts of constraint, but rather as the presence of alternatives for action, it might seem paradoxical that liberty should be of value. After all, one can never exercise more than one of several mutually exclusive options. The other alternatives are forever abandoned and unused. How can a path that I do not take make any more contribution to my life than people who were never born or paintings that the artist died too soon to paint? The purpose of this chapter is to show just why liberty, with its "unused alternatives" is valuable; both intrinsically and instrumentally. In addition, I will argue that social liberty receives a special justification from considerations of justice.

26. THE CONSEQUENCES OF LIBERTY

At least part of the answer to the "paradox of the unused alternatives" is simple and obvious. While I can pick only one alternative, the fact that I can pick *any* one, of many, typically leads to better consequences than if I had no choice. When I say "better consequences," for the time being, I intend those consequences that involve differences in the world outside the agent's own mind. These differences in the external world may, of course, lead to different subjective states for the agent, and this may be the chief (or only) source of their value. What I want to exclude, temporarily, are the immediate subjective consequences of liberty, including a feeling of mastery at having chosen one's own way. I will refer to all consequences except these immediate subjective consequences as "external."

It is a necessary (though not sufficient) condition of liberty's having desirable external consequences that the alternative I select, at least sometimes, be different from the one that would have been thrust upon me by the system of unfreedom. This is a very minimal assumption. It is, presumably, impossible to design any unfree system that would duplicate exactly what people choose in a system of considerable positive liberty. (This is not quite as obviously the case for a system of negative liberty, since it is theoretically possible for such a system to offer but one "alternative" at every point; the other possibilities being foreclosed by conditions other than direct human interferences.)

A second, and more interesting, assumption required by most consequentialist arguments for freedom is that people will tend to choose what is in their own interest more often than would even a benevolent authority. Choosing better is obviously more difficult than mere choosing differently. Still, letting people choose a great deal for themselves is surely the most effective practicable method of making choices which turn out to be satisfactory to the people involved. This line of argument is vulnerable, however, to the contention that there are specific and well-defined areas in which authorities are likely to make better choices than would the individuals themselves. Some have thought these areas to be numerous and extensive. If so, this particular consequentialist argument might properly justify only a limited freedom.

A different traditional consequentialist argument for liberty runs along the following lines. Liberty encourages diversity. (This is, of course, especially true of liberty positively conceived.) Diversity brings about competition which winnows out less desirable alternatives in favor of more desirable alternatives. When the diversity is in the realm of ideas and theories, the effect ought to be that the more plausible theories tend to gain acceptance over less plausible theories. Assuming, as we must, that the more plausible theories are statistically more likely to be true, freedom of ideas and expression should tend towards the acceptance of more truth than would a system of unfreedom. This generating and filtering procedure, familiar from Mill, is widely praised in the West under the somewhat misleading title "the free market-place of ideas." It is possible to think up situations in which this is not a good procedure for discovering truth, but in a wide range of settings, it deserves its good press.

The same generating and filtering procedure can also produce valuable results when applied to ways of life. If diverse experiments in community life are tried, some will no doubt lose their adherents and die out. Those that gain acceptance will make a direct contribution to value. That contribution will be a matter of external consequences, so long as people do tend to choose what is in their interest. It will inevitably be a contribution in terms of the immediate subjective rewards of having travelled one's own path.

There are also well-known efficiency advantages to be derived from letting people make their own choices. Other methods of decision making are usually more cumbersome and forego motivational advantages. People typically do better work, for example, when they choose their own line of work.

Whatever these desirable tendencies, the ultimate rating of systems of freedom, in terms of their consequences, must remain a matter of a wealth of contingent facts about the world. For this reason, there is room for almost endless controversy over the sort of social system which would have the best consequences. In particular, there are many arguments which can be made against the consequential value of liberty. Some of these come in for mention in the next chapter. There are abstract models of benevolent dictatorship which claim advantages over systems of liberty, at least in terms of happiness. But we have good historical reasons to doubt the translatability of such models into practice. Their idea of happiness is also suspect. Moreover, there is a very widespread opinion that liberty *is* useful. It seems likely that this opinion is grounded on a pretty good insight into the complex contingent nature of things.

There remains some question, however, whether a justification in terms of consequences could possibly be given for the exact structure of positive liberty as developed in Chapters IV and V. Do the consequences of having alternatives really get better and better as the number of alternatives grows larger? Isn't there, perhaps, some large number n such that, if there are more than n alternatives, the consequences actually get worse, because we are tempted either to spend too much time deciding or to use slipshod methods of deciding?[1]

Another potential problem arises with trivial and degrading alternatives. These will count as increasing positive liberty in terms of both the number and the difference of alternatives. This increase in liberty may be deflated to a very low level by considerations in the "value" family. But why should trivial and degrading alternatives be counted positively at all? In terms of the most obvious sorts of consequentialist reasoning, they seem clearly undesirable. If they are actually chosen, they have their undesirable consequences. If they are not chosen, they will at least have occupied some deliberation time, which could have been better spent in some other way.

There are utilitarian replies to this utilitarian argument against positive liberty. One of them involves the familiar problem of social epistemology that what seems to nearly all of us to be trivial or degrading may, in fact, be the key to the good life. For specific delimited classes of acts, however, we can probably be as sure that they are not keys to the good life as we are that the earth is not flat. In such cases, the considerations so far examined would permit prohibiting the alternative.

Perhaps a sophisticated consequentialist morality could justify positive liberty as characterized in Chapters IV and V; given enough favorable contingencies. I have some doubts about this project if the consequences are restricted to the external. Immediate subjective consequences present the possibility of a special consequential argument about which I am more optimistic, as will emerge shortly.

However well consequentialist arguments in favor of liberty may fare, it is also of interest whether liberty is intrinsically valuable, as some philosophers and political leaders have asserted, but other philosophers, including some strong supporters of liberty, seem not to believe. In examining this question we will have the opportunity to take a closer look at the question of trivial and degrading alternatives.

27. INTRINSIC VALUE DEFINED

It is a tricky business to try to establish the intrinsic value of anything. Is justification or argument possible here at all, or are we inevitably thrown back upon direct intuition? Moral obligations, rights, and permissibilities may be entailed or made plausible by other features of the moral system. This, at least, puts a step or two between what is being justified and pure intuition (or stipulation). Instrumental values are justified by their consequences. but if something is intrinsically valuable, mustn't its value come from within itself? If its value is not a matter of its relation to anything else, however, we cannot expect to argue from anything else to the existence of that value. Bearing this in mind, we will be well advised not to be more demanding than we need be of the "intrinsically valuable." This point is reinforced by the observation that on some strong readings of "valuable for its own sake," almost nothing will have this property. Pleasure, for example, is presumably not valuable for its own sake, but for our sake.

Obviously, then, a great deal will turn on exactly how "intrinsic value" is defined. My own definition, I think, corresponds to one traditional way in which this phase has been understood, but not to others. I shall take intrinsic value to be any value that is not instrumental. By an instrumental value, I mean one that is valuable entirely by virtue of its causal consequences. So whenever something has value independently of the value of its causal consequences, that value is intrinsic. Or, if you subtract from the total value of something that value it has by virtue of its causal consequences, what remains is its intrinsic value.

This notion of intrinsic value is in some respects a weak one. For example, it does not have the consequence that what is intrinsically valuable is valuable in isolation or in every context. Something might be intrinsically valuable in one context and of no value, or even of negative value, in other contexts. Perhaps intrinsic values are more interesting if they are also independently valuable and universally valuable, but it is of considerable interest that something is valuable non-instrumentally. It seems to me that the philosophical discussion of value has often gone wrong by conflating or confusing these different matters, and as a result losing sight of values which are not both universal and independent but also not instrumental. Liberty falls into this category. It is not, in any strong sense, "independently" valuable. It is, I think, universally valuable, though only on a weakened notion of universal value. And, while it has valuable consequences, it is also valuable non-instrumentally or, as I will say, intrinsically.

28. THE INTRINSIC VALUE OF AUTONOMY AND LIBERTY

My general strategy in arguing for the intrinsic value of liberty is to show that it is a non-causal necessary condition of an intrinsically valuable complex and contributes value to that complex. The heart of the valuable complex in question is personal autonomy. Autonomy, even together with all its parts and relations, is not the only valuable thing, but it is something of considerable value. Before examining why the autonomy complex is valuable, let me review what I intend by "autonomy."

Autonomy is making one's own choices. A person is not autonomous whose choices are dictated "from outside" at gunpoint or, perhaps, through hypnosis. One may also not be autonomous when one chooses under the influence of certain massive "internal" compulsions or personality disrupting influences. On the other hand, full deliberative rationality is not required for autonomy. Spontaneous or ill-considered decisions can be just as much *my* decisions, and that is the touchstone as I understand autonomy. The autonomous person is one who goes his or her own way.

It is tempting to try to construct an argument for the value of autonomy from the fact that autonomy is central to our moral system. Very impressionistically, one might reason as follows. The moral system is either the source of or reflects moral value. Without autonomy, there could be no moral system, at least in anything like its present form. Such notions as "right and wrong," "obligation," "human right," and "permissibility" obviously make sense only in the context of choices. Autonomy and the capacity for autonomy qualitatively increase the moral standing of an individual. One who is non-autonomous cannot be subject to obligations. One who is not even potentially autonomous does not have the rights of autonomous or potentially autonomous individuals. (Presumably this is at least part of the reason we believe animals can be subject to conditions which would count as slavery for human beings.) Since it is necessary for the existence of moral values, autonomy must itself be valuable. Alternatively, since it contributes to the moral status of individuals, autonomy must itself be valuable.

There may be a good argument in this neighborhood somewhere, but I confess I cannot find it. Obviously, not everything that has a major role in shaping the structure of our moral system is valuable. Consider the existence of wickedness. Then too, the capacity to feel pain increases the moral status of an individual. (That is why we can do things to artichokes we cannot morally do to armadilloes.) But the capacity to feel pain, especially intense and continuing pain, is of dubious intrinsic value.

It is, I think, of significance that autonomy is so central to our moral system and qualitatively enhances the moral dignity of individuals. But its value comes from the specific way it fits into human life and contributes to moral dignity. It does not have value simply by virtue of the fact that it is a central moral category.

To look to the details of human autonomy is to look to such matters as creativity, risk taking and avoiding, resisting and succumbing to temptation, holding to principle, compromising, admitting mistakes, sacrificing oneself and sacrificing others, and struggling through in the face of adversity. The list is, of course, incomplete. The first thing to be said about the autonomy complex is that the world is obviously a richer place because it contains autonomous beings. This is, I think, already a plus. Abstractly considered, worlds having this sort of diversity on the moral plane are much more interesting. Other things being equal, one would want to live in an interesting world rather than a dull one.

The larger share of the value of the autonomy complex comes, however, not from its diversity and richness but from the value of some of its individual components. Creativity, for example, is clearly valuable. It may be that non-autonomous beings or machines can create; certainly computers can produce novelty. But creativity through autonomous choice is a process that is worthy of respect, even if its results could be duplicated in some other way. Creativity is not valuable simply for its effects. We rightly admire it for itself.

Similarly, we value for themselves many acts of risk taking, holding to principle, sacrificing, compromising, admitting mistakes, and struggling through. These are, or can be, instances of what is most admirable in people. We value them in many cases where their consequences are negligible or even unfortunate.

Of course, these positive components of the autonomy complex have their opposite numbers. We do not always do well with our choices. If there could be no heroic following of principle without autonomy, there could also be no cowardly depravity. I am not going to claim that there is more herosim than cowardice as a matter of fact, nor even that heroism has historically "out-weighed" cowardice. I do think that the risk of cowardice is worth taking for the possibility of heroism. Slavish imitation is a risk worth taking for creativity. Some of the components of the autonomy complex represent the chance of rising to a high level of excellence and humanity. We treasure this chance even though we frequently fall short.

I want to call special attention to the process of choosing that is central to the autonomy complex. This process is, I think, itself valuable, even when the choice is not a good one. A mental life without choice is very much poorer than one with choice. Deliberating, choosing, exercising one's rational judgment are often pleasurable, but, even when they are not, they are desirable forms of consciousness. In all cases of choice, one rises above a passivity and injects something of oneself into the world. Many cases of choosing are, in addition, complex and demanding; calling for intelligence, concentration and strength of will. The desire to make choices is, again, a desire to manifest some of the "higher" potentials of human beings – those which seem most significantly to set human beings apart.

In examining the non-instrumental value of the autonomy complex, I have inevitably referred to desire and desirability. I take it that 'x is desirable' is, on its more formal reading, equivalent to 'x would be desired by a rational and informed person' or 'x ought to be desired by a rational and informed person.' To be desirable is, then, either the same thing as to be valuable, or a close relative. Desire, on the other hand, is a psychological state. Its presence or absence is an empirically ascertainable matter of fact.

It is subject for debate, which I want largely to avoid, just what relation desire has to desirability and value. But I want to suggest the following principle which will, I hope, be uncontroversial at least on my definition of intrinsic value:

If A desires x at least partly for properties of x that are not matters of x's causal consequences, and if those properties are not such that A ought not to desire x, then x is intrinsically valuable for A.

We desire to be the sort of people who choose, are creative and courageous, and putting causal consequences aside, there does not seem to be any reason why we ought not to have these desires. They involve desires for autonomy itself which is a non-causal precondition of choice, creativity, courage, and the like, and relying on the "best possibilities" argument, it is not the case that we ought not to have these desires for autonomy.

Liberty is valuable because it is a non-causal precondition of autonomy. Without something to choose, one cannot go one's own way. Since, excluding causal consequences, there is no reason one ought not to desire liberty and since, in the absence of such reasons, it is rational for the desire for autonomy to extend to this necessary condition, liberty is itself intrinsically valuable.

It might be thought that we do not need real liberty and autonomy, but that a sufficiently good counterfeit would be just as valuable. One might feel as good about oneself if one thought that one had creatively proved an important theorem while, in fact, one had acquired someone else's proof through subliminal means.

But I take it that what we desire is really to be creative rather than simply to think we are. (In fact, this latter sort of desire is hard to imagine anyone actually having; unless as part of an exercise in confirmation of a philosophical doctrine held for other reasons.) In general, it is rational to want to have an excellence, a property that contributes to self respect, rather than simply to have the appearances, even if the appearances are perfect and there is no danger that we will be disabused of our beliefs. Not to care whether one actually has an excellence, so long as one thinks one does, is an odd attitude to adopt towards oneself. Certainly there is no reason of the intrinsic sort, *not* to desire really to have such excellences as creativity or courage or autonomy itself. I conclude, then, that autonomy and the freedom on which it depends, are intrinsically more valuable than their perfect counterfeits.

For those who do not, on reflection, share my desire for real freedom as against its appearance, I would have to fall back upon the following argument. First, the appearance of freedom is valuable. Second, the only workable way to have the appearance of freedom for any length of time (outside of science fiction cases) is really to have freedom.[2] Positive liberty would then be an instrumental value, but an instrumental value of a special kind. The existence of alternatives would have as causal consequences the desirable states of consciousness associated with the autonomy complex, including feelings of self worth, and of the possibility of excellence. These valuable consequences freedom would have before and independently of its consequences through the effect of choices on the world. In short, the value of liberty would be independent of the external consequences with which such traditional arguments as Mill's have been mostly concerned. So even if I were wrong that freedom is intrinsically valuable, its value would still be more immediate and less a function of the contingencies of the world than utilitarian accounts have usually suggested.

29. VALUE AND THE STRUCTURE OF POSITIVE LIBERTY

I want now to strengthen my conclusion that liberty is intrinsically valuable by showing that the greater the liberty, the greater the value, other things being equal. Given the possibilities embraced by "other things," it will not always be true that greater liberty leads to a *net* increase in intrinsic value. But liberty does have a tendency to increase value. It always makes a positive contribution, though it may also sometimes make a greater negative contribution. This is what I meant above when I said that liberty is universally valuable, but in a weak sense.

To verify the weak universal value of liberty, I will first run through the structure of positive freedom as analyzed in Chapter IV, showing how each of the variables that increases freedom tends to increase the value of the autonomy complex as well. I will then turn to an objection to my thesis about the intrinsic value of liberty. The objection focuses on depraved actions, where it may initially seem as if, contrary to my claims, liberty makes only a negative contribution.

To begin the survey of the correlation between positive liberty and value, it seems plausible that an increase in either the number or diversity of alternatives should increase the scope for autonomy. In defining oneself against a larger range of possibilities more is risked, but, by the same token, the achievement is greater. More space is available for deliberation, imagination and creativity. Even depraved options contribute unambiguously to value when they are successfully resisted.

The next variable determining the degree of liberty is the probability of realizing the alternative if one attempts it. Recall that low probability may bear on the value of the alternative either positively or negatively. But independent of value, low probability always deflates the contribution to liberty of the alternative. Rationally, we must think of an improbable alternative as only a partial alternative. Obviously, then, it contributes less to the scope of autonomy and to the value of the autonomy complex. (In addition, its instrumental value typically suffers, since the more desirable consequences usually flow from success rather than from failure.)

An increase in the "value" of alternatives, as characterized in Section 14, also contributes to the value of autonomy – not surprisingly. The loss of an alternative that I have already chosen is a direct blow to autonomy as, to a lesser extent, is the loss of an alternative I have had under serious consideration. Similarly, gaining an alternative that is a serious candidate expands the effective area for my choice and control more than does the addition of an alternative I would not think twice about. (There ought to be a positive correlation with instrumental value as well. It is the alternatives that seem most desirable that are most likely to contribute to my actual future well being.)

This completes my survey of the correlation between positive liberty and intrinsic value and completes, as well, the "value foundations" argument for positive liberty. By showing that positive liberty has intrinsic value and that the intrinsic value of liberty increases with increases in the defining variables of positive liberty, I have shown that, from the perspective of basic moral theory, liberty is positive liberty. That is, when we look to what makes liberty intrinsically valuable, and project from that the scope of liberty, we do not have to make an extension to get positive liberty. Rather, we have to make a restriction to get negative liberty. As suggested in the Introduction, this value foundations argument extends and deepens the "moral similarity" argument with which the last chapter was largely concerned. It gives a more fundamental reason for doubting the moral importance of the differences between negative account preventing conditions such as restraint and positive account preventing conditions such as incapacity and poverty.

Let me now turn to the objection mentioned above. Depraved actions are typically worse when they are done freely rather than, for example, under coercion. The vicious torturing of an animal is surely more reprehensible if the torturer had numerous alternatives of value. Since autonomy and liberty make such actions worse rather than better, neither can be intrinsically valuable.

I am sure that the reader will have anticipated my first reply to this objection. From my standpoint, it conflates intrinsic value and universal value. Compatible with my definition of intrinsic value as non-instrumental value, I could simply admit that liberty and autonomy are not intrinsically valuable in the context of depraved actions, while they are intrinsically valuable in (most) contexts of creative or courageous actions. However, as indicated above, I do want to claim that liberty is universally valuable in a weak sense. It makes some positive contribution to value in any context, even if, all things considered, net value diminishes with an increase in liberty in some contexts.

When we think about an action like the vicious torturing of an animal, our evaluations typically focus either on the wrongness of the action or on the moral depravity of the agent as reflected by that action. We usually are less interested in other features of the whole state of affiairs except as relevant to judging the agent or the action. This may seduce us into the too quick conclusion that, where the action is depraved, that agent's autonomy makes only a negative contribution to the whole state of affairs.

In the torturing case, the agent's autonomy renders both the agent and the action worse than they would otherwise be. But are we to conclude, on these grounds, that the autonomy itself was of negative value? If we so conclude, we count for nothing the positive possibilities of the autonomy complex. This would be to say that the chance to grasp excellence or goodness loses all value if one fails to make the best of the chance. The intrinsic value of autonomy, via its valuable possibilities, such as creativity and courage, does not make the action or the agent morally better. But it is better, in a morally relevant sense, that a choice situation should be autonomous rather than non-autonomous. (That this value does not necessarily transfer to the value of the action is no more surprising than that a valuable gun does not make better a murder committed with it.)

What I have just given is my chief argument for the value of autonomy, and the value contribution of liberty, in the case of a depraved act. It relies heavily on the value of unactualized possibilities. While this seems to me to be sound, I have a second argument for those who are unsure. It turns on what I think is a less significant way in which autonomy and freedom contribute some positive value in the case of depraved actions.

We may admire the cleverness of a fiendish crime, while believing that the cold premeditation it bespeaks renders the crime that much more heinous. Cleverness is itself a member of the autonomy complex; either a form of, or related to, creativity. Not all depraved actions exhibit cleverness or creativity, of course. But all autonomous actions, however depraved, are done by choice. And, as already discussed, choice, by itself, is a good thing in exercising higher mental capacities. In this respect, the presence of choice adds at least a slight positive element to any action.

It may also be true, though I am unsure about this, that it is always a good thing taken in isolation that a human being get what he or she has chosen. If it is true, then any successful carrying out of an intention is in that respect good, though it may be bad given the content of the intention. Suppose we hear that Samantha, of unknown character, has gotten her way about something, we know not what. I am tempted to respond, 'Well, at least it's good that she got her way.' But one might also respond, 'Whether that's good or bad depends on what she got her way about.' The latter is clearly a correct response, but I am doubtful that its correctness shows that the first response is incorrect. If not, then, we have another positive value contribution which autonomy and liberty make to (successful) depraved actions.

30. AN EGALITARIAN ARGUMENT FOR POSITIVE LIBERTY

I have argued that liberty has instrumental and intrinsic value. I want now to argue that there are considerations of justice between persons which militate in favor of a system of high positive liberty.

Consider Timothy who lives in an authoritarian society with strict limitations on freedom of speech, association and movement. One is not free to choose where or when one is to work or where one is to live. Higher authorities determine how much education one receives, what one reads, and, indirectly, much of what one thinks.

As it turns out, however, Timothy could not be happier. He is ideally suited to the work he does, and is well thought of by his peers and superiors. There is no place else he would rather live. He had just as much education as he wanted. He would not read books on the banned list, even if they were encouraged rather than banned. The social and religious opinions which are proscribed are ones he finds detestable anyway. In short, there is almost nothing that Timothy would be doing differently in a free society.

Compare Timothy's case now with that of his compatriot Ursula. Ursula's education was cut short against her will. She is forced to work at a job which she dislikes, in a town she finds boring. She would eagerly read some of the banned books, if she could get her hands on them, and would denounce the regime but for the fact it would land her in jail.

Obviously, Ursula's situation is bad and should be condemned on all sorts of grounds. But, for present purposes, I am only interested in the comparison between the situations of Timothy and Ursula. It is true, in one respect, that Ursula can do everything Timothy can. But we obviously do not want to conclude that the system places them in an equal position with respect to liberty. The negative libertarian should be quick to point out that Ursula is interfered with at every turn, while Timothy's wishes are never thwarted. Now I would not want to conclude from this that Timothy is free and Ursula not. In terms of positive liberty, Timothy is somewhat freer than Ursula, since the alternatives open to him he desires more than she does the opportunities open to her. But, whether one believes in positive liberty or not, it is clear that Ursula is disadvantaged relative to Timothy. Timothy does what he wants, Ursula cannot.

There will typically be cases like that of Timothy and Ursula in any unfree society. Some people naturally swim with the stream, other do not. In all such cases, the dissidents can validly complain that they are unfairly treated in comparison to the others. That some should be able to do what they want while others are prevented from doing so, is a fundamental inequality. Where the restrictions in question have a major role in shaping everyday life, this inequality looms so large that, on this basis alone, the authoritarian society must be considered unacceptably unjust.

This argument for the injustice of unfreedom depends on the contingent fact that some people will find the content of a given set of restrictions quite compatible with their desires and way of life, while others will find themselves enormously frustrated. The argument does not assume any of the conclusions of the previous sections of this chapter. It only requires two principles from the side of ethical theory. First, being frustrated at every turn in one's day to day life constitutes a fundamental disadvantage in comparison to one who is not frustrated. Second, a system which fundamentally disadvantages one person as compared to another is unjust and hence morally unacceptable.

This is a weighty argument in favor of liberty, but one would not want to depend upon it alone. It is not applicable to an authoritarian society whose manipulation of people's minds is so successful that no one wants to do anything but just what the authorities ordain.

In the absence of such manipulation, the argument cuts, not just against restrictions in negative liberty, but also against societies whose positive social liberty is significantly lower than it could be. A person with a correctable physical incapacity will usually be in a position to do many fewer of the things he or she would like to do than is a person without such incapacity.

CHAPTER VIII

THE COSTS AND LIMITS OF LIBERTY

Since liberty is not the only thing of value, there are times when it comes into conflict with other values. Let me use the phrase 'the costs of liberty' broadly to include any case where we have less of something else of value because we have more liberty. Sometimes the costs are too high and liberty must be reluctantly curtailed. In other cases, liberty should be defended despite its costs. It is impossible to canvass all the potential costs of liberty. But an account leaves the standing of liberty vague if it does not say something about which costs are properly taken as sufficient to restrict liberty. This topic has come up here and there in previous chapters; it is time to take a more systematic, though inevitably still very inexhaustive, look at it.

31. DECISION COSTS

When we think of the costs of liberty, we normally think first of the personal and social consequences of bad decisions. But there is one kind of cost which may be unacceptably high even when the decision arrived at is the right one. These are "decision costs," costs of gathering information and weighing alternatives as well as the psychic costs of worrying about the decision before and after it is made.[1]

Consider, for example, the conscientious consumer who cannot make any significant purchase without checking out all the published test reports, discussing the matter with experts, making charts and tables, weighing advantages and disadvantages, and so on *ad nauseum*. (Ignore, for present purposes, the fact that many conscientious consumers enjoy these activities. Think of the ones who do it out of duty or the fear of being taken advantage of.)

If life's alternatives were dramatically broadened, as suggested by the positive libertarian social program, there would be a danger that many of us would feel like conscientious consumers with too much money. We would be overwhelmed by the mass of significant decisions bearing down upon us. Aren't we, perhaps, better off with fewer options which can be examined with reasonable thoroughness and about which we can have some confidence that we have made the right choice?

I will argue that where they arise as a policy issue, decision costs warrant restricting alternatives only in those cases where decision procedures are less than fully rational. If I am right about this, restricting alternatives because of decision costs will, if justified at all, be justified on what may loosely be called "paternalistic" grounds – which will be the subject of the next section.

In examining the question of decision costs, let me assume (contrary to what was shown above) that liberty has neither intrinsic value nor consequential value of what I have called the "immediate subjective" sort. That is, I will take the value of liberty to lie solely in the probability of choosing a better alternative than one would have chosen with less liberty. This assumption, obviously, makes it more difficult to show that the liberty of a rational agent should never be restricted because of decision costs.

A first and fairly easy question about liberty and decision costs is this: when will the addition of new alternatives to a choice set produce no net loss? This will happen just in case:

$$(v_1 - c_1) \le (v_2 - c_2),$$

where v_1 is the utility of the alternative that would have been selected from the original choice set; v_2 is the utility of the alternative that would be selected from the choice set with the addition of the new alternatives; c_1 is the decision cost of choosing from the original choice set; and c_2 is the decision cost of choosing from the enlarged choice set. I do not assume that v_2 is the result of selecting one of the new alternatives. After the addition of new alternatives, we may make the same selection as we would have made from the original choice set, or we may select a different "old" alternative. I do assume that $c_1 \le c_2$, so if it were to happen that $v_1 = v_2$, there would be, at best, no gain in having the additional alternatives. Under these assumptions, there can be little doubt that gaining new alternatives will sometimes mean a net loss.

But we do not yet have the problem in the proper form for the policy issue raised by the possibility of restricting the alternatives of a rational decision maker because of decision costs. What the decision maker must work with is not utilities but expected utilities. (If all the actual utilities were known in advance, decision costs would all but vanish.) So let v_1' and v_2' represent, respectively, the expected utilities of the alternatives chosen from the original and from the enlarged choice sets.

Now suppose a legislature is considering whether to lift a ban, thus expanding our rational agent's choice set. Clearly, there is no harm in doing so, so long as:

$$(v_1' - c_1) \le (v_2' - c_2).$$

Now whether this inequality will hold would seem, in part, to be a matter of how "fertile" the new alternatives are in comparison to the old; that is, how rich each set is in alternatives with high expected utilities. To be more precise, choice set X is more fertile than choice set Y relative to decision procedure D if the expected utility of applying D to X is greater than the expected utility of applying D to Y. X is more fertile than Y if the expected utility of applying the best (for X) decision procedure to X is greater than the expected utility of applying the best (for Y) decision procedure to Y.[2] Notice that the less fertile set may have the best alternative, so long as the set is large enough that one is unlikely to find it. Fertility is a matter of the best alternative one is *likely* to turn up.

Obviously, if the new alternatives are more fertile than the old, they should be added. (I assume the old alternatives cannot be dropped.) If the new set is equal in fertility to the old, there is no harm in the addition. So let us consider the worst case for liberty vis à vis decision costs, the case where the new alternatives are less fertile than the old. When one is searching for a needle in a haystack, the last thing one wants is more hay. The next to last thing one wants is more needles, if they come with more hay and are less well represented in the new hay than the old needles were in the old hay.

To deal with this case, let me distinguish two kinds of decision procedures. An exhaustive procedure considers all the alternatives in the set. A non-exhaustive procedure will stop before considering all the alternatives, if the expected utility of going on to look for a better alternative is outweighed by the decision cost of doing so. Obviously, it is rational to use a non-exhaustive procedure when one is available. (What is irrational about some (overly) conscientious consumers is precisely their unwillingness to adopt non-exhaustive strategies.)

Moreover, a non-exhaustive procedure *is always* available (unless one is under some outside compulsion to use an exhaustive procedure). The expected utility estimates may be rough and intuitive, but they can always be made. (And we do make them all the time. 'What is the likelihood that I will find, in the next month, a house whose purchase is enough more attractive . . . ?')

Given a non-exhaustive decision procedure, there is no problem in our inequality's holding, even in the case of adding a set of less fertile alternatives. One simply adds them to the end of the list of alternatives. Perhaps the decision procedure won't reach them. If not, there is no increase in decision costs. If the procedure does reach them, it can only be because it is rational to try them for a while. Expected gain outweighs decision costs.

This assumes that the maker of the decision can distinguish the new alternatives from the old. It is one thing for more hay to be piled ten feet away from the needle hunter's haystack. It is another thing for new hay to be mixed into that haystack. But the case under consideration is where someone, say the legislature, *can* distinguish the less fertile choice set from the more fertile set, since it bans (or considers banning) the less fertile set. In this case, instead of banning the less fertile set, the legislature could simply make available the information as to which alternatives are members of which set. In the case of commercial products, for example, it could require a warning label on members of the less fertile set. With this information available, the rational decision maker armed with a non-exhaustive decision procedure will not ever be a loser, in terms of expected utilities, from having a wider rather than a narrower set of choices.

Of course, not everyone is rational about their decision procedures. But before we resort to restrictions on liberty, we should at least insure that we have taken other steps more appropriate to the problem of the not fully rational management of decision costs.

Perhaps education in the proper way to handle decisions would be the most fruitful means of coping with the problem. In addition, we could require all those who offer products, services, education, and jobs to do a better job of informing the public. If moderately detailed and reasonably objective information were available, it would significantly reduce the research time of the overly conscientious. In addition, we might institute "decision counselors" or even "binding decision counselors." The latter one would go voluntarily, but once one had turned a decision over to them, one would have to abide by their determination. Then there is always the possibility of psychiatric help for those whose problems with decisions are symptomatic of other problems. Given the availability of these various ways of dealing with decision costs, it is unlikely that these costs would ever constitute a sufficient reason to limit liberty, even for less than fully rational agents. But if they seemed to, we would be confronted with the issue of paternalism.

32. PERSONAL COSTS AND PATERNALISM

It is a fact of life that people sometimes make decisions that have bad consequences for themselves. On some occasions, it seems morally permissible to intervene to prevent the agent from making or carrying out a bad decision, limiting the agent's liberty for his or her own sake. In the largest and most important class of such cases, the agents in question are children. I take it as a given that children and people who are seriously misinformed about the nature of their actions may sometimes be interfered with, even though their actions do not threaten harm to anyone else. I want to consider what justifies this sort of interference and how far it is justified.

Traditionally, these interferences are called "paternalistic." Let me explain how I understand paternalism by defining first "paternalistic intent" and then "purely paternalistic" action.

An action by A which limits B's freedom is done with *paternalistic intent* if and only if it is part of A's intent to benefit B by limiting B's freedom.

I would take "contribute to B's welfare" or "contribute to B's good" to be substitutable in this definition for "benefit B."

An action by A which limits B's freedom is *purely paternalistic* if and only if A has no intent in limiting B's freedom that is not paternalistic.

As has been often noted,[3] purely paternalistic actions are relatively uncommon, and purely paternalistic enactments of law are very uncommon. In particular, laws against risky activities will not be purely paternalistic if the lawmakers were in part moved by considerations of the welfare of the risk taker's family or associates or of the risk taker's potential social contribution or of the fact that the disabled risk taker might draw upon public assistance. To narrow the scope of the inquiry to purely paternalistic limitations might, then, be to limit it too far. On the other hand, to consider all cases where there is paternalistic intent is to deal with such a mixed class that there is danger of missing what is unique about the problem of paternalism.

What I will focus upon are those cases in which paternalism may be thought to *justify* limitations of freedom that would not otherwise be justifiable. So the question is under what circumstances considerations of the agent's own welfare contribute essentially to a morally proper justification of a limitation on that agent's actions.

My answer will be that paternalism, as defined, never contributes to the justification of the limitation of the agent's actions. This is essentially the position made famous by Mill.

... the only purpose for which power can be rightfully exercised over any member of a civilized community, against his will, is to prevent harm to others. He cannot rightfully be compelled to do or forbear because it will be better for him to do so, because it will make him happier, because, in the opinion of others, to do so would be wise, or even right.[4]

While I would express it somewhat differently, I think that what Mill intends here, though radical and far reaching, is absolutely right when we are speaking of people who pass minimum standards of moral agenthood.

As critics have often observed, it is impossible to get Mill's unqualified position on paternalism from a utilitarian argument. Radical anti-paternalism can only come from the view that respect for a person's autonomy requires us to give that agent's choice strict priority over his or her own welfare. As Feinberg puts it:

> If . . . our ultimate principle expresses respect for a person's voluntary choice *as such*, . . . we can remain adamantly opposed to paternalism even in the most extreme cases of self-harm, for we shall be committed to the view that there is something more important (even) than the avoidance of harms.[5]

I think that according this priority to autonomy is morally correct. I suspect that it is ultimately to be defended in terms of a contractarian or semi-contractarian understanding of morality. (There is nothing in the functioning of a public morality that would require the individual to cede to that morality a say over his or her actions so far as they affect only himself or herself.) Obviously, there is room for more discussion of the moral foundations of this principle, but that would be a long inquiry into the foundations of morality. What I will do instead, along with other recent defenders of anti-paternalistic positions, is to show that embracing anti-paternalism does not run us into insurmountable problems with our intuitions in particular cases. The challenge is to find, in those cases in which it seems clear that we ought to intervene, non-paternalistic grounds for doing so.

Cases in which people have intuitions that intervention is called for include the following: preventing an infant from toddling over a cliff, a ten year old from riding a bicycle on the freeway, an unwary pedestrian from setting foot on an unsafe bridge, and a temporarily despondent person from committing suicide. More controversial, but still claiming considerable intuitive support, are requiring motor cycle helmets and banning the use of heroin and cigarettes.

I want to talk about three different strategies for permitting at least some of these interferences while holding to an anti-paternalistic position. The three can be called the "third party" strategy," the "disqualified agent" strategy, and the "consent" strategy.

It is often easy to find third party reasons to interfere with what seems at first a "self regarding" action. In the case of the ban on heroin, for example, it is argued that the social costs of heroin use are held down (somewhat) by laws against its use. Keeping the bicycle off the freeway has an even clearer third party justification. Given social funding of health care or public assistance to the incapacitated, all the cases mentioned can be given third party justifications. But if third party justifications are easy to come by, it is not at all clear how much weight they should be given. (The general issue involved here, the social costs of liberty, will be discussed next section.) Moreover, third party justifications are not very interesting theoretically. They do not seem to go to the heart of the matter. Surely, third party considerations are not the chief source of the intuitions that intervention is permissible to stop the toddler or the bridge crosser.

So far as I have been able to determine, every anti-paternalist relies at some point on one or another version of the "disqualified agent" strategy. This strategy starts out from the indisputable premise that a principle justified in terms of respect for autonomy will not apply to a subject who would not be autonomous even if we did not intervene. In the case of most animals, that of very young human beings, and that of people acting under coercion, we tend to think that interfering with their behaviour is not interfering with a significantly autonomous choice. Therefore, the anti-paternalistic principle ceases to apply.

On Feinberg's version of this strategy, it is only the agent acting *voluntarily* who is shielded from interference by the anti-paternalistic principle. The use of this version of the strategy, of course, requires getting reasonably clear on a standard of voluntariness, and this, as Feinberg grants, is not easy. If we are too lenient in counting actions as voluntary, we may not be able to intervene where we intuitively should. On the other hand, if the standard requires a great deal before it counts an action as voluntary, the anti-paternalistic principle itslef may become very weak. Feinberg's characterization of the fully voluntary assumption of a risk seems in danger of falling into this second pitfall.

One assumes a risk in a fully voluntary way when one shoulders it while fully informed of all relevant facts and contingencies, ... and in the absence of all coercive pressure of compulsion. There must be calmness and deliberateness, no distracting or unsettling emotions, no neurotic compulsion, no misunderstanding. To whatever extent there is compulsion, misinformation, excitement or impetuousness, clouded judgment (as e.g. from alcohol), or immature or defective faculties of reasoning, to that extent the choice falls short of perfect voluntariness.[6]

Under this characterization, it is very plausible that we ought not to interfere paternalistically with any fully voluntary action. For example, are we ever fully informed of all relevant facts and contingencies?

Fortunately, Feinberg does not regard full voluntariness as a necessary condition for a bar on paternalistic interference. In fact, we may interfere only with an action that is "substantially non-voluntary." Unfortunately, we are not given much help in grading degrees of voluntariness and involuntariness.

For Feinberg, the disqualified agent strategy does a great deal of work. It is the heart of what he calls "weak paternalism." But we can, and I think should, put less burden on this strategy in favor of a version of the third strategy.

Many have noticed that consent to interference sometimes constitutes an exception to the anti-paternalistic principle. Recently, Gerald Dworkin[7] and Rosemary Carter[8] have given quite different treatments of consent, but both take it to be the central exception to the moral bar on interfering for the sake of the agent.

Carter's account places the main burden on actual consent. It is uncontroversial that prior consent on the part of the agent to one's interfering in his or her affairs is usually sufficient for the interference to be permissible. It is especially likely to be sufficient where the agent would score higher on the voluntariness standard when giving the consent than when the interference takes place. And this is typical in prior consent cases.

Since actual prior consent is given in only a very small number of cases of intuitively justified interference, something else is needed if this general strategy is to play much of a role in making anti-paternalism compatible with our intuitions. Carter adopts "subsequent consent" (with conditions against brainwashing and the like). This extends the scope of the strategy considerably. But there are still too many cases that slip by: cases where the agent, for one reason or another, fails to give the subsequent consent that he or she would have been willing to give, or would have been willing to give with further information. So Carter adds a clause covering the case where, subsequent to the interference, the agent "is disposed to consent either upon request, or upon the receipt of a relevant piece of information."[9]

This seems to me to be close to the proper account, but there is still, at least theoretically, a problem. The agent, immediately after the interference, may die or become severely incompetent or undergo a major personality shift. To catch such cases, there seems to be no option but to follow Dworkin in embracing "hypothetical consent" (though like Dworkin and Berlin, we ought to be sensitive to the abuses to which hypothetical consent principles can lead). Cautiously formulated and used, a hypothetical consent strategy will, I think, cover most of those cases where it seems clearly justified to interfere for the sake of the agent. And it will do so without giving up anti-paternalism. The hypothetical consent principle I suggest is as follows:

(HC) A is justified in preventing B's doing x if A has good reason to believe that if B were in a state of deliberative rationality and had A's information, B would choose that A intervene to prevent B's doing x.

Let me make some comments on this principle. Notice first that, unlike typical forms of the disqualified agent strategy, HC is not even conditionally paternalistic. We are not allowed to intervene to *benefit* someone as such, rather we are allowed to intervene to bring about what he or she *would choose*. That is to say that we may intervene out of a consideration for someone's intentions but not, if this is different, out of a consideration for his or her real interest, as we understand it.

For example, A might grab B's jacket to keep B from dashing out the door if A realizes that B has forgotten B's cigarettes. A knows that getting the cigarettes is not in B's real interest, but feels an obligation, knowing that B would not choose to go off without the cigarettes.

The hypothetical consent principle also has a built-in restriction against interferences that are too irritating or too injurious to the agent's self respect. We are not allowed to intervene to prevent A's doing x just because A, if deliberatively rational and with our information, would choose not to do x. We are allowed to intervene only if, under these circumstances, A would choose that *we intervene* to stop A's doing x. In cases where the reasons for not doing x are lightweight relative to the negative features of the intervention, the intervention is not justified. If we know that A places a great deal of value on not being interfered with, we will rarely, if ever, be permitted to intervene.

Now let me say a little about the one obvious problem for the hypothetical consent account – characterizing the hypothetical "state of mind." The basic idea is that deliberative rationality is not to involve any fundamental "reform" in the agent's personality. It does not discount desires, however neurotic, unless they are intuitively temporary "alien" desires (for example, manipulatively induced desires) or are desires which exist solely as the result of faulty calculation (where a faulty calculation violates a principle of logic or mathematics or violates an elementary rule of decision theory or plausible theory construction). The deliberatively rational state is an abstraction from the actual present state of mind of the agent and differs from that actual state only with respect to the mechanics of decision making and some devaluation of desires in conflict with the agent's more permanent desires and purposes. Then, in addition to being deliberatively rational, the hypothetical mental state has all the information (justified belief) of the potential intervenor, insofar as such information is relevant to the decision.

Obviously, this is only an impressionistic initial description of the "mental state" appropriate to the hypothetical consent principle. I will not try, in this essay, to give it a more rigorous formulation, but I will do a little of the spade work for such a formulation by examining some applications of HC. This will also give us a chance to compare HC to approaches turning on actual consent and on voluntariness.

Consider Mill's famous case of preventing someone from walking out onto an unsafe bridge. On the voluntariness approach, we note that the intervenor has reason to believe that the pedestrian is not fully informed and that, as a result, there is a description of the action that the pedestrian is about to perform under which it is substantially non-voluntary. That description is "walking onto an unsafe bridge."

The problem is that we are never *fully* informed about any action. Most actions have some unknown and undesirable consequences, such that a description of the action in terms of those consequences might plausibly be associated with non-voluntariness. For example, by attending a colloquium, I will unwittingly expose myself to a virus which will give me a serious cold. Certainly, I exposed myself to the virus non-voluntarily, though I didn't go to the conference non-voluntarily. Now suppose that you know that in attending the colloquium I will expose myself to the virus. Suppose further that you have good grounds for believing that I do not know this. Ought you to intervene to stop me from going to the colloquium (perhaps by grabbing me as I rush to catch the last train that will get me there)?

If you try to make your decision whether or not to intervene in terms of Feinberg's voluntariness standard, the question will be whether my ignorance of the virus renders my behavior substantially non-voluntary. But what is substantial? HC suggests a solution to this problem. The action is substantially non-voluntary by virtue of my ignorance just in case I would want you to intervene to stop me from going to the colloquium if I were deliberatively rational and had your information. (And this will presumably turn largely on the relative importance to me of attending the colloquium versus remain healthy over the next week.)

I don't think anything other than this suggestion is plausible. Certainly we would not want to define "substantially non-voluntary" in such a case so as to permit intervention where the informed agent would disapprove of the intervention. Nor, I think, would we want to rule out intervention, by the voluntariness standard, where the agent would want to be interfered with. So in this case, the voluntariness approach reduces to the hypothetical consent approach.

Let me try to reinforce my contention that the voluntariness strategy, to be plausible, must, in many cases, be understood in terms of hypothetical consent. Consider the following case. Violet is listening in at the switchboard as her employer, Walter, conducts important negotiations by telephone. Walter, as Violet knows, is very drunk. Violet considers breaking the connection and jamming the switchboard to bring a temporary halt to the negotiations. As she listens to the conversation, Walter makes some agreements that Violet believes are not in his best interest, but none of them falls significantly below the usual standards of Walter's business decisions. Violet has good reason to believe that Walter, when sober, will not be too upset about the agreements made and would not want her to interfere by breaking the connection.

If the voluntariness standard has force independently of hypothetical consent, it would seem that it would license Violet's breaking the connection. Walter's behavior is intuitively substantially nonvoluntary and would apparently so count on Feinberg's standard. Moreover, it is not in his own best interest. The hypothetical consent (and subsequent consent) approaches would, however, forbid the intervention, as seems the proper anti-paternalist position. Having broken the connection, Violet would have no satisfactory defense against a sober Walter who demands, 'What right had you to break the connection if I, sober and in your place, would not have?'

Let me now consider three cases involving prior consent. A has B's consent to pull cigarettes from B's mouth and snuff them out. There is currently a cigarette in B's mouth. A considers an attack on the cigarette, for B's own good. In case (1), B was somewhat inebriated when the consent was given. In case (2), the consent was given a long time ago. In case (3), B's recent behavior suggests a reassessment of B's position on the question of cigarettes. In any of these cases, it seems that the question A ought to ask is 'Would B *now* consent to my plucking away the cigarette (if deliberatively rational)?' Even prior consent given when roaring drunk licenses intervention; if there is good reason to believe that the agent stands by it. On the other hand, consent given with the greatest sobriety and solemnity will not license "paternalistic" intervention if there is good reason to believe that the agent would not now stand by it in a state of deliberative rationality.

So, as with the voluntariness standard in the above cases, actual prior consent, to be plausible, is dependent upon hypothetical consent. Actual subsequent consent is liable to similar problems, especially if the period between intervention and consent is very long or the agent has gone through important personality changes. Hypothetical consent at the time of intervention will be the more appropriate test. "Dispositions to consent" are, as mentioned above, close to hypothetical consent. But using dispositions would be inferior for our purposes, because irrelevant circumstances may intervene to prevent the formation of the appropriate dispositions.

It would be possible to let a general anti-paternalistic principle stand together with HC as a complete solution to the problem of paternalism. We can, I suppose, apply hypothetical consent reasoning even in the case of infants and animals. This would, however, be strained. Especially in the case of animals, it is plausible that hypothetical consent would have to be interpreted simply in terms of the animal's welfare. So I propose the "disqualified agent" strategy for those cases where it is artificial to speak of an agent. Under these circumstances (rare for human beings), benefitting the subject will justify interferences with the subject's behavior. This will not be paternalism as such, since we will not be interfering with liberty. Liberty requires a decision maker with some sort of autonomy.

I hope I have made it plausible that we can embrace a strict anti-paternalist principle, in the spirit of Mill, without running into flagrantly unintuitive results. A limited use of "disqualified agency" permits some paternalism, but only where no autonomy is thereby diminished. Hypothetical consent allows interferences with an autonomous decision, but only where the agent would consent to the interference; surely a limitation on autonomy that is pre-eminently respectful of autonomy. In the case of adults, these principles will license very little interference. For the most part, people ought to be allowed to make bad decisions insofar as they affect themselves.

33. SOCIAL COSTS

One person's liberty often has undesirable effects on another person, and a system of liberty has costs for the society as a whole, because of its conflicts with other social ideals. A complete account of the moral status of liberty would give principles for deciding when these costs are acceptable and, conversely, when liberty must be limited. This task seems to me to require too much attention to specifics to be carried out in an essay like the present one. There have been principles proposed which are simple and comprehensive enough to give a general solution to the question of the limits of liberty. But none of these principles can, I think, be accepted. Let me examine a few of them.

The cleanest answer to the problem of the costs of liberty is that liberty must never be diminished because of its social costs. This is pretty obviously not going to work for liberty considered in the positive way, since the maximization of positive liberty is an open-ended enterprise capable of demanding ever greater sacrifices elsewhere. Not surprisingly, then, the idea that liberty is never to be curtailed has usually gone together with a restricted negative account of liberty.

On one cautious variant of this position, liberty is characterized as such a modest ideal as to make it nearly impossible for it to step on any important toes. One person's liberty is taken to end where that person risks harming or interfering with another person. Liberty so conceived may be without social costs, but it is a very limited liberty. There are few things that we do that do not affect someone detrimentally to some degree. The decision to drive to work contributes to traffic congestion and air pollution. Walking to work, one's presence on a crosswalk slows down a motorist. The clothes I wear or the sound of my voice may irritate people. Only when I sit quietly alone in the mountains can I be fairly sure that I am not causing anyone any harm – assuming that I do not harm by omission! So the "no harm" account of liberty is impossibly restrictive when taken seriously.

Perhaps, however, we are not really intended to take the account this seriously. For "harm" it might be more charitable to read "significant harm." This reading broadens the scope of liberty. But just what liberty is becomes nebulous. How much harm does it take to be significant? Does this vary with other matters, such as the importance of the liberty? Defining liberty in terms of the absence of significant harm does not solve the problem of the permissible limits of liberty. It simply relocates that problem. The structure of liberty itself must be made to bend and twist in relation to moral considerations arising from completely outside such matters as alternatives and interferences. If pornography is significantly harmful, then not only may pornography be prohibited, but to do so is no restriction of liberty! The alternative of causing a significant harm makes no contribution to liberty and interfering with it does not diminish liberty. This makes the account of liberty complex and *ad hoc*. In addition, there is a tendency for such accounts to slip into a total identification of liberty with morally permissible liberty. If we do this throughout, we get the unwelcome consequence that no one ever has more liberty than he or she should have, and the convicted felon does not lose liberty when imprisoned.

There is another problem with characterizing the limits of liberty in terms of the absence of significant harm. The relation of the permissibility of an action to the harm it causes others is complex and turns less on the seriousness of the harm than on the exact way it comes about. I may be greatly harmed if you successfully compete with me for a job. On the other hand, I may be harmed very little if you punch me in the nose. Yet you are morally permitted to compete for the job and not permitted to punch me in the nose (without provocation or the like). Obviously, one of the factors that makes a difference between the two cases is your legitimate interests. But this matter of legitimate interests itself resists any simple resolution in terms of harms and benefits. You do not have a legitimate interest in punching me in the nose, even if the pleasure this act gives you is very much greater than the pain caused me. On the other hand, you do, usually, have a legitimate interest in competing for the job, even if having the job makes much less contribution to your life than it would to mine. (You do not care about job's location, and have nearly as good a job already. If I do not get the job, I will have to sell my house, move, and settle for a very much less desirable job.) Obviously, then, what is and is not permissible depends on a great deal more than the severity of the harm caused.

Similar examples dispose of the slogan that liberty, or permissible liberty, extends to the point where it interferes with the liberty of another. Liberties can come into conflict, and you sometimes ought to be free to restrict my liberty.

The principle that liberty should be restricted only for the sake of liberty suffers the same fate. I ought not to be free to cause a brief and non-debilitating but significant pain (say, by using a voodoo doll), even if neither the pain nor the fear of the pain causes you to change, in the least, your actions or your reasons for acting. By putting liberty prior to considerations of welfare, Rawls suggests that, under favorable social conditions, liberty should not be limited except for the purpose of increasing or equalizing overall liberty. This is, however, only intended to be a first approximation principle for the basic institutions of society. I doubt, in fact, that the priority of liberty extends quite that far, but present considerations show, at least, that it does not extend to all individual actions.

By stating liberty principles in terms of "equal liberty," Rawls calls attention to the fact that equality is a separate value, quite distinct from liberty, and one which cannot properly be entirely subordinated to liberty. As discussed in Section 18, the maximization of positive libery is unlikely to lead to large inequalities in liberty. But such inequalities might appear and constitute a cost too great to accept.

Similarly, happiness and achievement are independent values. They might come into conflict with liberty over such issues as a guaranteed income for those who choose not to work. There is little to be gained by trying to argue in the abstract that happiness is more important than liberty or liberty more important than happiness. Certain liberties must not be sacrificed for certain kinds of happiness, but, by the same token, certain kinds of happiness must not be sacrificed for certain liberties.

The recognition that liberty must sometimes give way to other values, and that there is no simple formula for deciding conflicts between liberty and these values, ought not to lead to the conclusion that liberty may be lightly abandoned. There are strong and growing tendencies leading to liberty's being sacrificed far too quickly. Restriction is frequently direct, cheap, and administratively convenient. So it is best to approach a conflict of values with the presumption that liberty is to be sacrificed only in cases where the costs of liberty are very considerable and it is demonstrable that no liberty-preserving policy will sufficiently defray those costs. Arguments for curtailing liberty, or failing to expand liberty, should always be examined with a searching skepticism.

Obviously, there are many things of value, in addition to those mentioned above, which have potential conflicts with liberty. Among them, democracy must be singled out for special attention. A developed system of individual liberty requires a restriction on the range of decisions made socially through democratic procedures. So liberty has a cost in terms of democracy. The tension between liberty and democracy gives rise to many of the pivotal issues of political philosophy; rich in theoretical and practical implications. In the final section of this essay, I will take a quick look at some of these issues.

34. INDIVIDUAL DECISION AND COLLECTIVE DECISION

Liberty and democracy are allied values. Part of the moral justification of democracy is that it represents the most consistent workable extension of individual control over alternatives into the realm of social decision. Moreover, any genuine democracy requires a significant amount of individual liberty.

Nonetheless, liberty and democracy are two different things and can come into sharp conflict. People can democratically decide to restrict their own liberty or the liberty of a minority. And a maximum system of individual liberty might have little or no room for collective decision making. So liberty and democracy are potential rivals, the one claiming decisions for the individual which the other claims for society. How this conflict ought to be resolved is the topic for this final section.

I will not argue here, but will simply assume that, for reasons of autonomy, most collective decisions ought to be made democratically. So the question about the proper line between collective and individual decision making will be nearly equivalent to the question of the proper scope of democracy. Actually, there are two questions here. The first is *where* the line between individual and collective decision ought to be drawn. The second is *who* ought to draw that line for a given society, and by what procedure. I will take these up in turn.

An extreme collective resolution of the first question is to decide democratically all those decisions that affect more than one person. For reasons of the sort considered last section, this policy would leave little or no scope for individual liberty. In a wide range of cases, decisions ought, properly, to be made by a particular one of the persons affected – often, but not always, the person performing the actions with which the decision is concerned. (Presumably there are also some situations where the person who ought to make the decision is not among those affected by it, as in the case of wills.)

At the individualist extreme is the contention that all decisions should be individual decisions. There is no proper sphere for public decision making. Nozick suggests that once all properly private decisions are made, there may not be any choices left to make.[10] I want to pause to examine this contention, because it does represent, at least in abstraction, a maximally libertarian position.

I can find no ground to think that private decisions properly exhaust all decisions, even if Nozick's general theory about individual rights and property rights is correct. Consider a simple case. Xavier, Yvonne, and Zachery are shipwrecked on your traditional (unowned) desert island. There is only one large tree on the island which, you may imagine, our three protagonists all see simultaneously, prune simultaneously, and so on. In short, none of them has priority with respect to anything which might be taken to constitute acquisition of rights to the tree, under the "first come" principle dear to the hearts of some followers of Locke.

Now it turns out that there is a disagreement over what to do with this tree. Yvonne suggests it be cut down and made into a dugout in which to escape the island. Xavier contends it ought to be left in place to provide shade and a place for a signal flag as they wait, and hope, for rescue. Neither Xavier's nor Yvonne's individual rights take precedence over those of the other two. So if Zachery sides with either, there seems no moral grounds on which the dissenter can claim that the majority will should be frustated. In this case, then, individual decision ought to give way to democratic decision.

To make the case for collective decision more difficult, suppose that all decisions were about physical objects (including human beings), and that all physical objects were individually owned (each person self-owned), ownership conveying strong control rights. Perhaps, then, there would be no room for democratic decision. But there is no guarantee that this would continue to be the case. On Nozick's entitlement theory, for example, I can, subject to one proviso, give what I rightfully own to anyone – which, I take it, includes any group, whether it contain two persons or all of society. If what I give is indivisible, then collective decision – plausibly democratic – will have to be exercised over it until it ceases to be jointly owned. Presumably I could even give something on the *condition* that decisions about it be made democratically. Liberty, it seems, upsets exclusively individual decision making.

Moreover, as has frequently been commented upon, there are some things which are not plausible candidates for individual ownership and about which unchecked individual decisions lead to conflicts. An example is the atmosphere, my choice to breathe clean air, and an industrialist's choice to burn dirty fuels. An individualistic solution involves no outright "regulation," but permits suits by those harmed by pollution. This does not, however, circumvent the need for social decision. For example, what sorts of harms are compensable, under what procedures? Who pays for injuries which show up after the polluter has gone out of business?

Many decisions, of course, have primarily to do neither with owned nor unowned physical objects, but with cooperative undertakings. Frequently, a democratic vote is the only fair way to make such decisions as whether someone should be permitted to join us on our safari. I conclude, for these reasons among others, that the extreme individualist position on the distribution of decisions is unacceptable.

If we can rule out both the extreme individualist and the extreme collectivist position, that still leaves a great deal of latitude for drawing the line between individual and collective decision making. Are there any acceptable principles which help to narrow the field? Here are some candidates:

(1) If *A* has a right to do *x*, then the decision whether or not *A* is to do *x* ought to be *A*'s.
(2) If a decision is rightfully *A*'s and *A* voluntarily agrees to let *B* make the decision, then the decision ought to be *B*'s.
(3) If *A* rightfully owns *x*, then *A* ought to make the decisions concerning *x*.
(4) Everyone should individually make the decisions about his or her own actions.
(5) Anyone significantly affected by a decision should share in making it.
(6) Anyone vitally interested in the result of a decision should share in making it.
(7) Where *A* is significantly more affected by, or interested in, the outcome of a decision than is *B*, then *A* ought, at least, to have a greater voice in the decision than *B*.
(8) Where a group has unanimously decided in advance to make collectively decisions concerning a joint undertaking or joint property, those decisions ought to be made collectively.

With the possible exception of (1), which is not very informative, each of these principles has fairly obvious exceptions. Still, each of them has some force in some contexts. They are principles that hold other things being equal. Again excluding (1), I can find no exceptionless priority rankings among these principles. Everything seems to turn on the details of the particular cases. The issues must be settled at a level of considerably less abstraction.

So the question *where* the line between individual and collective decision is to be drawn has to take into account concrete details. This turns out not to be such a disadvantage, given *how* and *by whom* the line should be drawn for a given society. The short answer to the latter question is that the decision about the division of decisions should itself be made democratically.

With respect to this meta-decision, there is simply no other appropriate procedure save democracy. The question is, in effect, a constitutional one: what is to be the reach of society acting collectively and what protected for the individual? The possibility that such constitutional questions ought to be dictated by any single individual is almost too absurd to consider. It is very little more plausible that the decision should be made by some group which does not embrace all the competent members of the society.

The best case for minority constitution making occurs when the minority can be reasonably sure that the constitution it imposes on the rest of society is the proper constitution. Assume, for the sake of argument, that it is possible that a constitution, or part thereof, can be morally correct, though not accepted by most of the members of the society. Other things being equal, it is always nice that the right decision be made: the one which corresponds to the moral facts. This is no less true for constitutional decisions.

Suppose that you and I know the moral score with respect to constitutional matters. Obviously, we ought to try to persuade everyone else to adopt our conclusions. but we might fail at that. The issues are after all complex, and perhaps we are not as persuasive as we might be. If we have the power, is it now permissible for us to impose our constitution on the rest of unenlightened society? Even though our constitution is morally correct, it is, I think, not permissible to impose it by undemocratic means, except in extreme cases. Under normal circumstances, the moral correctness of the design of basic social institutions and practices is not sufficient to institute them against the wishes of society.

It is presumably true that people would agree with us if they had all the facts and reasoned correctly. But idealized counterfactual agreement is not the same thing as agreement. Imposing basic institutions and practices upon people against their actual wishes is like imposing a way of life on an individual against his or her will. Even if what is imposed really is in the best or "highest" interest of the persons or persons involved, to impose it is insufficiently respectful of autonomy. So we can rule out the possibility that a minority, however wise, ought to make the decision about the dividing line between collective and individual decision.

Another possibility is that the decision should be made by everyone, but individually rather than collectively. Everyone might decide for himself or herself what decisions he or she is to make and what decisions are to be left for other individuals or for collective decision. The problem with this procedure is that it would almost certainly lead to conflict, unless everyone is very wise and very saintly. It is a fact of life that individuals frequently want to enlarge the reach of their own power. Two people will lay claim to the same decision, each asserting that it is properly his or hers alone. Similarly, an individual may lay claim to a decision which the rest of us believe ought to be settled collectively. Letting individual decision reign, then, would presumably fail to produce a unique solution to the question which decisions are properly whose. Individuals and society must be protected against the excessive claims of individuals. By elimination, then, we are led to non-minoritarian collective procedures.

It might be thought that unanimous consent is a superior procedure to majoritarian democracy in the resolution of these issues. And in one respect, of course, it is. Where it works, it protects everyone's autonomy. Unfortunately, unanimous democracy does not guarantee a decision. Unanimity is not always obtainable, especially in the sorts of conflicts I have been imagining. Majoritarian democracy does guarantee the decision in all cases. It gives maximum weight to individual autonomy of any procedure having this property. It is also, of course, the case that majoritarian decisions are more likely to be widely supported than decisions reached in less democratic ways. They create fewer "strains of commitment."[11]

For these reasons, democracy has a procedural superiority to other decisions methods. It is the procedure by which fundamental social questions ought to be resolved, including the question of the proper scope of collective and individual decision. It may seem as if giving democracy this procedural priority introduces an untenable asymmetry. Liberty and democracy are different values. Neither is reducible to the other (at least fully). There is no moral presumption that democracy has the stronger case when they conflict. So why let democracy adjudicate conflicts between the two? Isn't this like letting a person be the judge of his or her own case? But of course democracy is not a person or quasi-person. It does not have interests of its own, but simply reflects those of its constituents. It is as easy for the majority to decide a given case in favor of liberty and against democracy as it is for an individual. Democratic decisions need not be democratic decisions.

Let me emphasize that the procedural priority of democracy entails neither that a decision democratically arrived at is correct nor that the individual is absolutely obliged to abide by it. In particular, the democratic determination of the scope of liberty may take liberty away from an individual which that individual ought to have. Where this denial of liberty is sufficiently serious, the individual has a right to disobey and resist the democratic decision. This is not to retreat on the claim that the boundaries of individual liberty ought to be subject to democratic decision. The best available decision procedure creates a *prima facie* obligation to obey its results simply because they are its results. But this obligation may be defeated. The content of the decision actually reached and the conscience of the individual are of independent importance and may, in particular cases, exceed in moral weight the superior procedure.

So I conclude that decisions about liberty ought to be made democratically, where this is understood to be compatible with the possibility of some justified disobedience. Obviously, my arguments have just scratched the surface of a difficult area which has seen a good deal of intense and sophisticated work by political philosophers. The issues could and should be explored in much greater depth, but that would run to a length at least equal to that of the present essay. I do think I can defend the view that any political philosophy giving human autonomy a central place ought to accept my conclusion on democracy in constitution writing.[12] The alternative procedures risk either the despotic imposition of basic institutions and practices or endless conflict among individuals in which the weak would tend to lose power to the strong.

The conclusion that decisions about liberty ought to be made democratically is especially compelling where we understand liberty as positive liberty. A thinner and more formal liberty could be written into a relatively brief constitutional document. But positive liberty embraces so much social and economic policy that it inevitably involves detailed legislative decisions. There are few public decisions that do not affect the extent or distribution of positive liberty in one way or another. To substitute some other procedure for democracy in decisions involving positive liberty would be tantamount to abandoning democracy altogether, in favor of something less respectful of autonomy.

It is a corollary that a movement aimed at securing positive liberty must itself be a democratic movement. It need not be democratic in the sense of putting all its energies into the established electoral processes. In some societies, that would be suicidal; in others, it would be a bad strategy. It should be democratic in the sense of aiming to become the "independent movement of the immense majority, in the interest of the immense majority."[13] Anything less would be false to the centrality of autonomy that is revealed by an analysis of positive liberty.

NOTES

CHAPTER I

[1] Inaugural Lecture at Oxford, published by Clarendon Press, (Oxford, 1958). Reprinted in Berlin's *Four Essays on Liberty* (Oxford, 1969).

[2] It is not, however, clear that positive liberty, even positive liberty conceived as self determination, is especially liable to this distortion. It is easy to imagine a parallel distortion, guided by the same illogic and metaphysical excess, leading to tyranny in the name of negative liberty. This point is made by Marshall Cohen in "Berlin and the Liberal Tradition," *The Philosophical Quarterly* 10 (1960), 223.

[3] *Four Essays on Liberty*, 122.

[4] *Ibid.* 1iii.

[5] I deal briefly with the "autonomy as rationality" position in Section 9.

[6] "Negative and Positive Freedom," *Philosophical Review* 76 (1967), 312–34.

[7] *Ibid.* 314. This is similar to Felix Oppenheim's triadic definition of freedom in *Dimensions of Freedom* (New York, 1961). Oppenheim restricts his second variable to persons, however: X is free with respect to person Y to do Z. This restriction is incompatible with much of the positive account, and, as a result, with much of MacCallum's thesis.

[8] "Negative and Positive Freedom," 320.

[9] *Ibid.* 312.

CHAPTER II

[1] *Leviathan*, Chapter XXI, emphasis Hobbes'.

[2] *Ibid.*

[3] Hart, *The Concept of Law* (Oxford, 1959), Hart and Honore, *Causation and the Law* (Oxford, 1961). Nozick, "Coercion," in S. Morgenbesser *et al.* editors, *Philosophy, Science, and Method: Essays in Honor of Ernest Nagel* (New York, 1969). Reprinted in Lasle and Runciman, editors, *Philosophy, Politics, and Society*, 4th series. Page references to Nozick's paper, below, will be from this reprinting.

[4] See Nozick, "Coercion," 118.

[5] *Ibid.* 107.

[6] Perhaps this should include "subconscious intents."

[7] For example, William A. Parent in "Recent Work on the Concept of Liberty," *American Philosophical Quarterly* 11 (July, 1974), 156: "Perhaps feelings can be measured in degrees, but it is extremely doubtful whether unfreedom can be."

[8] "Coercion," 115. See also p. 112 for Nozick's discussion of "morally expected" outcomes.

[9] See Nozick, *Anarchy, State, and Utopia* (New York, 1974), 262.

[10] This assertion may depend on limiting the class of possible doings. For example, understanding "negative actions" (like not swimming) performable even by the dead, everyone is free to swim or not swim and everyone is free not to draw a round square. So let my claim that there is no absolute freedom to do anything be thought of as excepting negative actions.

CHAPTER III

[1] "Liberty and Equality," *Law Quarterly Review* 56 (1946), reprinted in *Political Philosophy*, Anthony Quinton, editor, (Oxford, 1967), 135, 136.

[2] Radio and television stations in the U.S. are not even required to *sell* time to candidates with whom they disagree. See *Columbia Broadcasting System v. Democratic National Committee*, 93 S.Ct. 2080 (1973).

[3] *Word and Object*, (Cambridge, Mass., 1960), 144.

[4] This principle is obviously false if extended to *relative* increases in the attractiveness of *x* by diminishing the attractiveness of the alternative. The robber's gun increases the relative attractiveness of handing over my wallet.

[5] *Second Treatise of Government*, Chapter VI.

[6] *On Liberty*, Chapter V.

[7] "Freedom and Government," in *Freedom, Its Meaning*, Ruth Nanda Anshen, editor (New York, 1940), 251.

[8] Inaugural lecture at Oxford, published by Clarendon Press, (Oxford, 1958), 7.

[9] *Four Essays on Liberty*, 122.

[10] "Liberty and Equality," 133.

[11] *Ibid.* 134.

[12] *Ibid.* 134–35, footnote omitted.

CHAPTER IV

[1] *Four Essays on Liberty*, 130.

[2] Low probability may contribute to an alternative's *value*, for risk seekers.

[3] See Section 31.

[4] It will be necessary (and not easy) to restrict alternative descriptions to those forms permitting enough identity among alternatives to yield these results. For example, if 'doing *x* on Tuesday' were a permissible alternative description, then it would never be the case that I can do everything today that I could do yesterday. And if '*A*'s doing *x*' is a permissible alternative description, it will never be the case that I can do all the things you can do.

[5] Russell makes this same point from the standpoint of a somewhat different account of freedom in "Freedom and Government," *op. cit.* 251.

[6] The fundamental objective probabilities for any alternative might well be either 0 or 1 – the determinists' thesis. Obviously, such an account of probability would be of no use for the present enterprise. It may be, however, that there is a way of defining probability independently of such epistemic matters as theory – even idealized theory – that would be more fitting for my purposes than is probability on the "best possible theory." For example, an objective probability guaranteeing alternative possibilities might be defined in terms of the actual (perhaps undiscoverable) laws of nature and possible worlds differing from the actual world only with respect to the agent's choices (and then, of course, the consequences of those choices). If such a probability can be defined, there would be good reason, I think, to take it as the real "objective probability" for the purposes of characterizing freedom. Where it conflicts with probability on the best possible theory, it would be because the best possible theory is not good enough. There are numerous problems in developing an account of probability along these lines. At best, it would take much more space than I could give it in this essay. If you believe that some such account of objective probability can be worked out, you should think of it as substituted in what follows for "probability on the best possible theory."

[7] I owe the idea for this formulation to Jane English.

CHAPTER V

[1] *Four Essays on Liberty*, xl. See also xlviii–xlix where "social and political liberty" is used to mark off human from non-human obstacles.

[2] *Ibid.* lvi.

[3] Berlin's account is in *Four Essays*, 130. See also my discussion of it in Section 11 above. For some of Berlin's relevant remarks, see Sections 21 and 22.

[4] This initial per capita grant would be understood as a final accounting of the secessionists' share of the social accumulation. Presumably, an individual could be counted only once towards such a grant; in case he or she should leave one community and later join another.

[5] *On Liberty*, end of Chapter IV. Other important discussions on self determinative secession can be found in the Marxist tradition, which has long recognized the rights of ethnic groups to secede. The restriction to ethnic groups seems to me unfortunate, since ethnic identification is so often accompanied by racist or chauvinist ideologies. Ethnic groups, as such, I think, ought to be discouraged from secession or even from segregating themselves. The community identification which ought to be encouraged is that based on agreement about a way of life, not that based on race or national background. In any event, secession should certainly be permitted no less for like minded individuals than for ethnic groups. (For an elaboration and defense of separate communities from a decidedly non-Marxist perspective, see the third part of Robert Nozick's *Anarchy, State, and Utopia*.)

[6] *On Liberty*, Chapter II.

[7] *Collected Works*, v. 25 (Moscow, 1964), 377–78.

[8] See my "Equality, Solidarity, and Rawls' Maximin," *Philosophy and Public Affairs* 6 (Spring, 1977), 262–66, for an egalitarian argument against maximizing the minimum level of primary goods.

[9] See Tony Cliff, *Russia: A Marxist Analysis* (London, 1970).

CHAPTER VI

[1] (New York, 1959), 248.

[2] *Ibid.* 248–49.

[3] *Social Philosophy*, (New Jersey, 1973), 9.

[4] *Four Essays on Liberty*, liii.

[5] *Ibid.*

[6] *A Theory of Justice* (Cambridge, Mass., 1971), 204.

[7] In *Reading Rawls*, Norman Daniels, editor (New York, 1974), 253–83.

[8] See *A Theory of Justice*, 127–28.

[9] *Four Essays on Liberty*, liv.

[10] (New York, 1967), v. 3, 22.

[11] As quoted in *Four Essays on Liberty*, 122.

[12] See Section 15, above.

[13] There is, however, a rival conjecture about the superiority of 'I am not free to fly like an eagle' over 'I am unfree to fly like an eagle.' Since "unfree" has more an official or serious sound than "not free," it may trigger legal associations which clash with positive uses.

[14] See Bruce Russell, "On the Relative Strictness of Negative and Positive Duties," *American Philosophical Quarterly* 14 (April, 1977), 93.

[15] A third condition ought to be added to get a characterization of human rights appropriate to the traditional debate over the existence of such rights:

The obligations correlated with the right are not simply obligations to maximize the social good, or some part of the social good, or to act in accordance with the recognition that each person's good counts toward the total social good.

For my purposes in this essay, however, there is no loss, and may be some gain, in considering the wider class of rights that result by leaving out this third necessary condition on human rights.

[16] See Nozick, "Coercion," 115.

[17] *Ibid.*

[18] *Anarchy, State, and Utopia*, 28–29.

[19] *Ibid.* 30–31.

[20] Perhaps paternalistic coercion is to be understood as *using* someone even though it is for his or her own benefit as an end. But it does not seem very natural to say that this "sacrifices" that person or uses him or her "merely as a means." My own view is that coercion is wrong, not primarily because it *uses* another, but simply because it restricts that person's autonomy. That much is a loss whether the person is used for the benefit of another, benefited by his or her own action, or coerced into doing something of no benefit to anyone. (Pointless coercion is a common feature of bureaucracies.) More on paternalism in Section 32.

[21] *Anarchy, State, and Utopia*, 32–33. Emphasis Nozick's; footnote omitted.

[22] Actually, this would depend on "their" theory of the single consciousness. It would not be incoherent for that theory to be that each of them participates in the joint consciousness, which participation will cease with the individual's death. 'The consciousness will roll on without me.' A theory along these lines might be supported by evidence about the way the group mind arose and about its physical basis. If the theory were accepted, there might be some prohibition on sacrificing an individual member's life. The issues here are intriguing, but large.

CHAPTER VII

[1] See Section 31.

[2] It is easy to have less freedom than one thinks one has. This may, in fact, be typical. What I am considering here is the extreme case of having no freedom: no alternative one is free to pursue. This entails complete non-autonomy.

CHAPTER VIII

[1] These decisions are emphasized as a cost of liberty by Gerald Dworkin in "More of Less: The Case of Choice."

[2] By the best decision procedure for X, I mean an (intuitively effective) procedure which, on the best available theory and evidence, has at least as high an expected utility in application to X as any other (intuitively effective) procedure. (I say "intuitively effective" to avoid ruling out procedures, if any, which always yield results for human beings, but, when spelled out, would fail more rigorous criteria for effectiveness. 'Pick the best alternative' is not intuitively effective. 'Pick the alternative you feel best about' might be.)

[3] For example, see Gerald Dworkin, "Paternalism" in *Morality and the Law*, Richard A. Wasserstrom, editor (Belmont, California, 1971), 117.

[4] *On Liberty*, Chapter I.

[5] "Legal Paternalism," *Canadian Journal of Philosophy* 1 (September, 1971), 120.

[6] *Ibid.* 110–11.

[7] "Paternalism." See especially 119.

[8] "Justifying Paternalism," *Canadian Journal of Philosophy* 7 (March, 1977), 133–45.

[9] *Ibid.* 136.

[10] *Anarchy, State, and Utopia*, 166.

[11] See *A Theory of Justice*, 145, 176.

[12] Democracy in constitution writing is, of course, in the end anti-constitutional, if one understands constitutions to have a special status as against ordinary laws. For constitutions to be protected from majority amendment, by super-majority requirements or waiting periods, is directly contrary to the arguments for majoritarian constitution writing.

[13] Karl Marx, *Communist Manifesto*, Section I.

MELBOURNE INTERNATIONAL
PHILOSOPHY SERIES

Other volumes in this series:

1. N. Rotenstreich, Philosophy, history and politics: studies in
   contemporary English philosophy of history. 1976. ISBN 90-247-1743-4.
2. J.T.J. Srzednicki, Elements of social and political philosophy. 1976.
   ISBN 90-247-1744-2.
3. W. Tatarkiewicz, Analysis of happiness. 1976. ISBN 90-247-1807-4.
4. K. Twardowski, On the content and object of presentations: a
   psychological investigation, translated by R. Grossmann. 1977. ISBN
   90-247-1926-7.
5. W. Tatarkiewicz, A history of six ideas: an essay in aesthetics.
   1980. ISBN 90-247-2233-0.
6. H.W. Noonan, Objects and identity: an examination of the relative
   identity thesis and its consequences. 1980. ISBN 90-247-2292-6.

Series ISBN 90-247-2331-0.